# THE LOCAL COUNCIL CL

# The
# Local Council
# Clerk's Guide

*by*

Paul Clayden

Shaw & Sons

*Published by*
Shaw & Sons Limited
Shaway House
21 Bourne Park
Bourne Road
Crayford
Kent DA1 4BZ

www.shaws.co.uk

© Shaw & Sons Limited 2001

Published January 2001

ISBN 0 7219 1600 7

A CIP catalogue record for this book is
available from the British Library

*Printed in Great Britain by*
MPG Books Limited, Bodmin

# CONTENTS

# Contents

# Contents

# Contents

# PREFACE

Hitherto, there has not been published (at least in recent years) a guide for local council clerks which is both succinct and practical. The present volume hopes to achieve these aims. Statutory and case references have been kept to a minimum, yet there are more than a hundred of them, thus indicating the many sources of law on which local council clerks need to draw in order to carry out their roles properly.

One of the difficulties which the writers of books on legal subjects face is that the law is constantly changing. As a result, a newly published book may be partly out of date almost as soon as it appears. In relation to this book, the Local Government Act 2000 makes a number of changes in the law which will directly affect local councils. The Act received Royal Assent in July 2000 but, at the time of going to press, it was not wholly in force and no date had been set for the implementation of Parts III and V which are of particular relevance to local councils and their clerks. So that readers are aware of the main provisions of these Parts of the Act, they are described and explained in Appendix 8.

Readers will note that clerks and councillors are referred to in the male gender. This is done purely for convenience and is not intended to detract in any way from the competence of female clerks. I am not alone in this practice; it is also adopted by the draftsmen of Acts of Parliament, no doubt because the English language has no single pronoun which applies to people of both sexes.

**Paul Clayden**
Henley-on-Thames
*November 2000*

# CHAPTER 1

# INTRODUCTION

The office and title of clerk are of venerable and honourable origin. The office of "parish clerk" pre-dates the establishment of civil parishes and parish councils by the Local Government Act 1894. The Act empowered the newly created parish councils to appoint a clerk, thus preserving the continuity of the title, although any constitutional connection with the Church of England was severed.

The clerkship of a local council may originally have been simple and undemanding, requiring few skills. This has not been the case for a long time. The job now calls for a high level of skill and commitment and should engender a commensurate level of job satisfaction.

This book covers the following areas –

❏ The role of the clerk, including agendas, proceedings at meetings, minutes, administration and correspondence, finance, management of property.

❏ Employment contract and job description.

❏ Qualifications, training and skills.

❏ The constitutional position and the role of local councils.

## Explanation of terms

Unless otherwise stated:

— the term "local council" refers to a parish council in England, a community council in Wales or a town council in both countries;

— the term "parish meeting" refers to a parish meeting in England, a community meeting in Wales or a town meeting in both countries;

— the term "the Secretary of State" refers to the Secretary of State for the Environment, Transport and the Regions;

— a reference to a district or a unitary council includes a reference to a county or county borough council in Wales.

## Explanation of footnotes

The footnotes give references to the Acts of Parliament and Statutory Instruments which set out the law relating to the relevant subject in the text. Some of the Acts and Statutory Instruments are given abbreviated titles. The full titles are as follows –

| | |
|---|---|
| AAR 1996 | Accounts and Audit Regulations 1996 |
| ACA 1998 | Audit Commission Act 1998 |
| ERA 1996 | Employment Rights Act 1996 |
| LGA 1972 | Local Government Act 1972 |
| LGFA 1992 | Local Government Finance Act 1992 |
| LGHA 1989 | Local Government and Housing Act 1989 |
| LGRA 1997 | Local Government and Rating Act 1997 |

## Abbreviations

The Society of Local Council Clerks (for address, see Appendix 5) is referred to as SLCC.

The National Association of Local Councils (for address, see Appendix 5) is referred to as NALC.

The National Joint Council for Local Government Services (for address, see Appendix 5) is referred to as NJC.

# CHAPTER 2

# THE ROLE OF THE CLERK

## 1. INTRODUCTION

The clerk's overall responsibility is to carry out the policy decisions of the council. He is akin to the chief executive of a principal authority, in that he is the head of the council's administration. He is almost invariably the council's "proper officer" (see Chapter 3 "Employment Contract and Job Description", below, page 53). Very often, too, he is the council's sole employee. He is responsible for seeing that the business of the council runs smoothly and efficiently and is conducted in accordance with the law. Normally, too, he is responsible for ensuring that the council's financial transactions are properly authorised and recorded. Most clerks, as sole council employees, also have to perform the clerical and secretarial tasks without which the council's business cannot properly be transacted.

As well as the foregoing, the clerk has the responsibility of guiding and advising the council on matters of law and procedure. He is not, however, expected to be an expert and he will on occasion have to seek advice himself on such matters. It is, of course, important that appropriate advice is obtained and given to the council before the council makes a binding decision on any matter.

Whilst the clerk has to carry out council decisions, he is not prohibited from making suggestions or putting forward views to the council as part of its decision-making process. The clerk usually has access to many sources of information and he should be able to tap these for the benefit of the council. However, the clerk needs to be careful not to seek to impose his personal views on the council and must expect that those views will not always be accepted. The clerk may disagree with a council decision, but he must carry it out to the best of his ability, unless the decision is obviously unlawful or beyond the council's powers. In such a case, he may advise the council not to proceed but, if his advice is ignored, he may have to resign his post. (See further "11. Initiatives and Guidance", below, page 49).

The administration of a local council's affairs is, in most cases, akin to the running of a small business. Thus most clerks work on their own, usually from home, and are free to organise their work as they think fit. They all need, therefore, the skills which are relevant to running a small business (as to which see Chapter IV "Qualifications, Training and Skills", below, page 87).

The detailed, day-to-day, work of the clerk is likely to fall into the following main areas, but with a good deal of overlap between them: agendas, meetings, minutes, administration, supervision of staff, finance (including investments), and management of property (including land and buildings, goods and chattels).

The final sections of this chapter deal with the relationships between the clerk and councillors and others, and initiatives and guidance on the part of the clerk.

## 2. AGENDAS

In order to make decisions and forward its policies, a council (and its committees, if any) must meet regularly. The responsibility for preparing the agendas for meetings and for producing the minutes of meetings almost invariably is that of the clerk. A few councils (mostly those with full-time clerks) have deputy clerks or committee clerks who also have this responsibility. Where the council has a large committee structure, it is in any event usually impossible for the clerk to be present at every meeting.

## General

The agenda specifies the business for a meeting. It is essential that the agenda includes all the items which are to be discussed at the meeting. The law provides that the business to be transacted at a council meeting must be specified in the summons to attend (i.e. the agenda), which means that the council cannot lawfully decide anything which is not on the agenda.[1] (For "Any other business" see below, page 14.)

The contents of an agenda are ultimately a matter for the council to determine. In practice, agendas tend to conform to a common pattern which reflects the continuing nature of much council business. An agenda will therefore usually comprise standard items (e.g. apologies for absence, approval of minutes, correspondence, accounts for payment), other matters of continuing business and items of new business. The clerk's responsibility is to include on the agenda on his own initiative any matters which are standard or continuing and any new matters which the council ought to consider. In addition, items put forward by councillors will need to be included as appropriate. It is not unusual for the clerk and the chairman to discuss the draft agenda for a meeting before it is finalised.

It is also very important that the agenda includes sufficient information to enable the council to discuss the items of business properly and to make sensible decisions about them. In preparing the agenda, the clerk should therefore bear in mind the following points:

---

[1]  Paragraphs 10(2)(b) and 26(2)(b) of Sch. 12, LGA 1972.

❏ Each agenda item should be fully described. For example, the item covering the signature of the minutes of a previous meeting should read "To sign as a correct record the minutes of the meeting held on [date]" and not simply "Minutes".

❏ Where necessary, the item should be accompanied by documentation containing essential supplementary information. For example, the item "Planning applications" should either include or have attached a list of relevant planning applications.

❏ Where a resolution is put forward by a councillor, the exact text of the resolution should be included. It may also be appropriate for the councillor to provide a written explanation of the background to the resolution and the purpose it is intended to achieve.

The format and appearance of the agenda should not be overlooked. An agenda prepared in a professional, businesslike way is likely to be appreciated by councillors and will certainly aid their discussions and decision making. Many computer software programs include standard layouts for agendas.

## Standard items

Whilst every meeting is unique, the agendas often have a great deal of similarity because much of the business which a council transacts is continuing business. There are a number of standard items which appear on many agendas and which should not be overlooked by the clerk. These are as follows –

❏ **Date, time and place of meeting.** These must by law be stated on the public notice announcing the meeting[2]

---

[2]  Paragraphs 10(2)(b) and 26(2)(b) of Sch. 12, LGA 1972.

and must in practice also be included in the summons to attend the meeting.

❏ **Apologies for absence.** This item is usually included because it provides a convenient means for a councillor who is going to be absent to give a reason. The need to give a reason for absence comes from the rule that a councillor who fails to attend a meeting of the council for six consecutive months automatically loses office unless, before the six month period expires, he gives a reason for absence and that reason is approved by the council.[3] Where an apology for absence is given, the clerk should seek to ensure that a reason for the absence is put forward so that the council can approve the reason, or not, as the case may be. If no reason for absence is given, there is nothing for the council to approve or disapprove and the six month period does not stop running.

❏ **Declarations of interest.** The law requires that any councillor who has a direct or indirect pecuniary interest in any contract, proposed contract or other matter which comes before the council must declare that interest and take no part in the discussion or voting on the matter.[4] The clerk is required to keep a book in which all declared interests must be recorded.[5] In addition, a councillor who is present at a meeting at which, broadly speaking, financial matters are to be considered, and who is more than two months in arrears with payment of his or her council tax, must declare the fact. He or she is not debarred from speaking but cannot vote.[6]

---

[3]   s. 85, LGA 1972.
[4]   s. 94, LGA 1972.
[5]   s. 96, LGA 1972.
[6]   s. 106, LGFA 1992.

As a reminder both to councillors and the clerk, some councils include a standard agenda item on the following lines: "To receive declarations of interest in accordance with section 94 of the Local Government Act 1972 [and section 106 of the Local Government Finance Act 1992]".

The law relating to the declaration of interests will be substantially altered when the relevant provisions of the Local Government Act 2000 come into force; see Appendix 8 for details.

❑ **Minutes of the previous meeting.** The law requires that the minutes of a meeting must be signed at the same meeting or at the next suitable meeting.[7] It is rare for minutes to be prepared and signed at the same meeting to which they relate. In practice, minutes are normally signed at the next meeting. They should be circulated in draft (i.e. unapproved) form, either soon after the meeting to which they relate or with the agenda for the meeting at which they are to be approved and signed. (For detailed guidance on the preparation of minutes, see below, page 22).

❑ **Matters arising from the minutes.** The purpose of this item is to enable items taken at the previous meeting to be up-dated (e.g. by the clerk reporting on action taken to implement a council decision). Since a good deal of council business is continuing business, there may be a tendency to deal with all matters relating to a particular item under this heading. The tendency should be resisted, because the council may find that virtually all its business is being taken under "matters arising from the minutes" and confusion may result. Confusion can be avoided by the matters for report being listed under the heading "Matters arising from the minutes",

---

[7]  Para. 41(1) of Sch. 12, LGA 1972.

and other matters being treated as separate agenda items. An alternative approach would be to avoid the phrase "matters arising from the minutes" and use some other phrase such as "matters for report".

❏ **Committee reports and recommendations.** Where a council has committees, it is essential that they report regularly to the council. Functional committees (i.e. committees with powers of decision delegated to them by the council) will normally report on their activities since the previous meeting. The reports can be written or oral. Non-functional committees (i.e. those with no delegated power to make decisions) will both report on their activities and place their recommendations (if any) before the council for approval. Whilst reports may be oral, recommendations should be in writing so that the councillors are aware of their exact nature.

The clerk should ensure that the relevant written reports and recommendations are attached to the agenda. It is common, too, for the minutes of committee meetings to be circulated to all councillors. However, it is not the function of the council to approve the minutes of a committee; that can only be done by the committee itself.

❏ **Chairman's/Town Mayor's report.** It is a fairly widespread practice for the chairman/town mayor to give an oral or, more rarely, a written report of his activities since the previous meeting.

❏ **Correspondence.** Councils tend to receive a great deal of correspondence and other documentation. It is the responsibility of the clerk to sort the wheat from the chaff and to report to the council those matters which are relevant. This is not always an easy task, because the categorisation of correspondence is to some extent subjective and the clerk may be criticised for not bringing before the council a matter which councillors regard as relevant and the clerk does not. To avoid criticism, some clerks arrange for every document received by the council to be reported and, sometimes, copied to all councillors. This is usually going too far and a middle way is preferable. Relevant letters and other documents should be reported under the specific agenda items to which they relate. Sometimes it will be appropriate to attach copies to the agenda. If there is no appropriate agenda item, it may be necessary to create one.

Caution needs to be exercised before correspondence is read out verbatim at a meeting or attached to an agenda. Letters of complaint, for example, may be defamatory and, if the council publicises them, it could become embroiled in legal proceedings. As a general rule, therefore, a letter should normally not be read out or copied; the clerk should give an oral summary of the point(s) made in it.

It will normally be helpful for the items of correspondence not being taken under other agenda items to be listed, with a brief indication of their subject matter. The clerk will need to have the items of correspondence to hand at council meetings in case reference to them is necessary. As a general rule, too, councillors have a right to inspect any letters and other documents which are relevant to the performance of their duties.

❑ **Planning.** Planning issues are perhaps the most important matters which come before most councils. It is therefore essential that the council has adequate information before it when discussing planning matters.

The council has a statutory right to be notified, on request, of the planning applications and decisions which relate to land or buildings in its area.[8] It is the duty of the clerk to ensure that sufficient details of all applications are circulated to the council or made available for inspection by council members. This is commonly done by attaching to the agenda a list of the planning applications received up to the date of issue of the agenda. (If the local planning authority supplies a list of applications received by it during a stated period, this can be circulated. However, the period covered by the list may be different from the period between the local council's meetings, a point which needs to be watched. The planning authority's list may also cover the whole of its area and not merely a single town, parish or community.)

Whilst it is not a legal requirement, most local planning authorities supply copies of all relevant planning applications and plans to the local councils in their area. It is usually not feasible to circulate these to council members, but the clerk should ensure that councillors have the opportunity to inspect them before the meeting at which the applications are to be considered. It is essential, too, that the applications and plans are taken to the council meeting for inspection/further inspection and reference.

There are many other planning matters which will come before the council from time to time. Of particular importance are structure and local plans, within the framework of which planning applications are determined. These, too, need to be discussed by the council at their various stages of consultation and preparation. It is the clerk's task to ensure that the

---

[8]  Para. 8 of Sch. 1 (England) and para. 2 of Sch. 1A (Wales), Town and Country Planning Act 1990.

council has the relevant information and documentation to enable it to make appropriate decisions.

❑ **Finance.** It is normal for every council meeting agenda to include a financial item. Usually between September and December, the council will set the budget for the following year and shortly thereafter decide upon its precept (which must be notified to the billing authority no later than 1st March).[9] Authorisation of accounts for payment will normally be required at every meeting and, at regular intervals, the clerk may need to produce a financial statement showing the current financial position of the council.

Where accounts for payment are to be approved, a list of the payments should be included in or attached to the agenda. The auditor will need to be satisfied that all payments have been properly authorised and a specific resolution by the council will ensure this.

❑ **Date of next meeting.** In England, a local council is required by statute to hold an annual meeting and at least three other meetings during the year (which runs from 1st April to the following 31st March).[10] In Wales, the council is required only to hold an annual meeting.[11] A council may, subject to the foregoing, hold as many other meetings as it chooses.

As a general rule, it is sensible for a council to set a programme of ordinary meetings for the year at its annual meeting. Many councils meet monthly, sometimes with a break in August. Others meet less frequently, either because the council is small and the

---

[9]  s. 41, LGFA 1992.
[10]  Paras. 7 and 8 of Sch.12, LGA 1972.
[11]  Paras. 23 and 24 of Sch. 12, LGA 1972.

volume of business does not justify more frequent meetings, or because the council is large and much of its business is delegated to committees.

In setting a programme of meetings, the council would be wise to have regard to the meeting programme of the relevant planning committee of the local planning authority. It should then be possible for council meetings to tie in with the meetings of the planning committee, thus ensuring that the comments of the council on planning applications are available to the planning committee at the proper time. This will usually mean that the council's meetings are held two to four weeks before the planning committee meetings.

❑ **Public question time.** It is common for members of the public to be allowed a period, usually before or after, but sometimes during, a meeting to raise questions or make comments. Whilst such a period is not in law a part of the council meeting, it is convenient to include a reference to it on the agenda.

## Non-standard items

The continuing nature of much council business will determine some of the non-standard items on an agenda. Others will reflect new business, including matters put forward by councillors. Yet others will cover procedural matters which arise on a regular or occasional basis, of which the following are most likely to be relevant –

❑ **Declarations of acceptance of office.** A new councillor may be elected or co-opted to fill a casual vacancy, or a new chairman/town mayor chosen otherwise than at the annual meeting. In these cases, the person concerned must sign a declaration of acceptance of office.

❑ **Exclusion of press and public.** The general rule is that council (and committee) meetings must be open to the public (which includes the press).[12] However, the council has power to resolve that the public be excluded for the whole or part of a meeting on the grounds that publicity would be prejudicial to the public interest, either because of the confidential nature of the business to be transacted or for some other stated reason.[13] Whilst not essential, it is helpful for such a resolution to be included in the agenda so that members of the press and public have advance warning that they may be excluded for the whole or part of a meeting.

A possible form of words for a resolution to exclude the public is:

"Pursuant to section 1(2) of the Public Bodies (Admission to Meetings) Act 1960 it is resolved that, because of the confidential nature of the business to be transacted, the public and the press leave the meeting during consideration of [here state the items of business]."

❑ **Any other business.** It is common practice for an agenda to contain the item "Any other business". As indicated above (page 5), the agenda must specify the business to be transacted at a meeting. The words "any other business" are too general to amount to a specification of business. Accordingly, the council cannot lawfully decide anything which is raised under such an agenda item, or indeed raised without proper notice. However, there is no legal objection to raising items of information, or matters for consideration at a future meeting, under "Any other business".

---

[12]  s. 1(1), Public Bodies (Admission to Meetings) Act 1960; s. 100, LGA 1972.
[13]  s. 1(2), Public Bodies (Admission to Meetings) Act 1960.

Whether or not to include "Any other business" on an agenda is ultimately a decision for the council. The author is of the view that the balance of advantage is against its inclusion on the ground that, if it is included, there is a danger that substantive decisions will be taken under that item which might be subject to challenge later. If the item is included in the agenda, another title may be preferable, such as "Matters for further discussion".

## Annual meeting

As indicated above, the council must hold an annual meeting. This must take place in May, save that in an ordinary election year it must be held within 14 days after the councillors come into office.[14] (This is usually in May as well, because the normal day for local council elections is the first Thursday in May.)[15] At the annual meeting, the procedural items of business will normally be –

❑ **Declarations of acceptance of office.** After election, every councillor must sign a declaration of acceptance of office in the prescribed form.[16] This is normally done at the first meeting of the council after the election. In an ordinary election year, that meeting will usually be the council's annual meeting. The clerk should have the necessary forms ready at the meeting.

The clerk should also have the declaration of acceptance of office for the newly elected chairman/town mayor to sign immediately after the election. If a chairman/town mayor is re-elected, he or she must sign a further declaration. This declaration is separate from the declaration a councillor signs on being elected to office.

---

[14] Para. 7 (England) and para. 23 (Wales) of Sch. 12, LGA 1972.

[15] s. 37, Representation of the People Act 1983.

[16] s. 83(4), LGA 1972.

❏ **Election of vice chairman/deputy town mayor.** The council does not have to elect a vice chairman/deputy town mayor but normally does so. The vice chairman/ deputy town mayor does not sign a declaration of acceptance of that office.

❏ **Appointment of committees.** It is a widespread practice for members of standing committees (e.g. finance, planning, environment) to be appointed on an annual basis at the annual council meeting.

❏ **Programme of meetings.** It is common practice for the council to agree upon a programme of meetings for the ensuing year, thus ensuring that all members know well in advance when council meetings will be held.

### Publicity

Agendas need to be suitably publicised so that members of the public and the press can readily find out when meetings are to take place and what is to be discussed. The law requires that copies of the agenda must be supplied to the press on request and on payment of postage or other necessary charge for transmission (if demanded).[17] It is a widespread practice, especially among large and medium sized councils, to send a copy of the agenda (if not all the supporting papers) to the local newspaper(s) without the need for a statutory demand.

The law also provides that meetings must be publicised by displaying a notice in a conspicuous place or places in the parish or community, giving the date, time and place.[18] There is no requirement that the agenda or business of a meeting is similarly publicised. However, it is clearly both

---

[17]  s. 1(4), Public Bodies (Admission to Meetings) Act 1960.
[18]  Para. 10(2) (England) and para. 26(2) (Wales) of Sch. 12, LGA 1972.

sensible and helpful if the agenda itself (but perhaps not the supporting papers, if any) is included in, or attached to, the statutory notice(s). The full agenda may also be placed in other public places, such as the local library or community centre, so that members of the public have a chance to inspect it before a meeting.

It is a good practice to have available copies of the agenda for the public at meetings so that they can follow the proceedings. The press should similarly be provided with copies of the agenda if this has not been sent in advance.

## 3. MEETINGS

As stated above (page 4), a council must meet in order to make decisions. Being a public body, largely financed by a compulsory levy on local residents (the council tax) the council must, as a general rule, meet in public.[19] If the public are to be excluded from the whole or part of a meeting, a specific resolution to that effect must be passed (see page 14 above).

The business to be discussed at a meeting is determined by the contents of the agenda, as described in the previous section. However, within those limits, there is considerable scope for diversity in the way in which the council handles discussion of agenda items.

### Calling of meetings

The statutory requirement for the calling of a council meeting is that three clear days' notice must be given by putting up a notice giving details of the date, time and place of the meeting in a conspicuous place or places in

---

[19]  s. 1(1), Public Bodies (Admission to Meetings) Act 1960.

the parish or community.[20] In calculating the three clear days, the day on which the notice is put up and the day of the meeting are not counted. Thus a meeting to be held on a Friday must be advertised no later than the previous Monday.

At the same time that public notice is given, a summons to attend the meeting must be sent by post or delivered to every member of the council, signed by the proper officer of the council (i.e. the clerk).[21]

It is the responsibility of the clerk to ensure that the statutory requirements relating to the calling of meetings are complied with. Additional publicity may be given (see above, pages 16-17) and is often desirable.

### Action before a meeting

Once the summons and agenda have been sent out, the clerk should make sure that all the information likely to be needed at the meeting is to hand. This may not all be in the clerk's possession at the time the meeting is called, in which case the clerk must try to make up any deficiency before the meeting takes place. Failure to do so may result in the council being unable to make a decision through lack of information and thus having to delay the matter until a subsequent meeting.

It is sensible not to delay the assembly of information until the day of the meeting, by which time it may be too late to obtain the information in time.

It is a common practice for the chairman and the clerk to meet and go through the agenda in good time before the meeting. The chairman can then be reasonably sure that

---

[20]  Para. 10(2) (England) and para. 26(2) (Wales) of Sch. 12, LGA 1972.
[21]  Para. 10(2)(b) (England) and para. 26(2)(b) (Wales) of Sch.12, LGA 1972.

he is properly informed about every item on the agenda and can plan the progress of the meeting. He, too, may have to seek further information before a meeting in order to be able to deal properly with agenda items.

It almost goes without saying that every councillor should read the agenda before a meeting and, if necessary, seek further information before the meeting takes place.

## Place of meeting

The clerk will need to ensure that a suitable meeting room is available.

The council may not meet on licensed premises unless no other suitable room is available either free of charge or at reasonable cost.[22] Otherwise the council may meet anywhere it chooses, within or outside the parish or community.

If there is no suitable room vested in the council which can be used free of charge, the council has a statutory right to meet in a school maintained by the local education authority, or in any premises which are maintained out of the rates (now the council tax). The council must meet any expenses (e.g. heating and lighting, caretaker's wages).[23]

Although not prohibited, it is generally undesirable for a council (or a committee) to meet in a private house because the council is conducting public business. The premises may also be unsuitable or not large enough to accommodate members of the public.

The meeting room must have reasonable access for disabled people.[24]

---

[22] Para 10(1) and 26(1) of Sch.12, LGA 1972.
[23] s. 134, LGA 1972.
[24] s. 19, Disability Discrimination Act 1995.

## Conduct of meetings

The conduct of a council meeting is primarily the responsibility of the person presiding, normally the chairman. He will be greatly helped procedurally by:

— the use of standing orders to provide a framework for discussion and decision making;

— thorough familiarity with the agenda items;

— the availability of guidance on legal and procedural issues from the clerk.

## The role of the clerk at meetings

The clerk has no direct part to play in the council's decision making. He has no right to speak or vote. His primary roles are to make a fair and accurate record of the proceedings and to advise the council on any matter which is raised at the meeting. In greater detail, the clerk's role is –

❑ To ensure that a quorum of members is present. The quorum (i.e. the minimum number present at a meeting to enable business to be validly transacted) is one third of the whole number of councillors, with a minimum of three[25] (e.g. 9 members, quorum 3; 10 members, quorum 4). However, where more than a third of the members are disqualified at the same time, then until the number of members is increased to not less than two-thirds of the whole number of members, the quorum is one third of the remaining members (e.g. 14 councillors, 5 disqualified: quorum 3).[26]

❑ To ensure that the council has proper advice on any

---

[25]  Para. 12 (England) and para. 28 (Wales) of Sch.12, LGA 1972.
[26]  Para. 45 of Sch.12, LGA 1972.

matter before it takes a decision, including matters of procedure. To be in a position to do this, the clerk needs to be equipped with the necessary tools for the job, such as proper training, relevant text books, etc. on legal and other matters, and other sources of information (for detailed guidance, see Chapter 4 "Qualifications, Training and Skills", below, page 87).

❑ To ensure that a sufficient note or other record of the proceedings is taken to enable accurate minutes to be prepared. Most clerks rely on manuscript notes which they, or more rarely a separate note-taker, make. Some make a tape recording and seek to use this in the preparation of minutes. The disadvantage of a tape recording is that it does not discriminate between the important and the unimportant. It may be difficult to distinguish between the formal decisions and other matters which must be included in the minutes and irrelevant matter.

The clerk would be well advised to retain the notes taken at meetings so that, in the event of the accuracy of the minutes being challenged, reference can be made to them. It is suggested that the notes on which minutes are based should be retained for about two years.

❑ To ensure that voting on decisions is properly recorded. Unless otherwise provided by the council's standing orders, voting is by a show of hands.[27] If the council holds a ballot in accordance with standing orders, the clerk must prepare the ballot papers and count the votes. A ballot may be open, where the ballot papers are signed by the councillors, or secret, where the ballot papers are unsigned. However, any councillor may

---

[27] Para. 13(1) (England) and para. 29(1) (Wales) of Sch.12, LGA 1972.

require that the voting on any question is recorded so as to show whether each member present and voting voted for or against the question.[28]

❏ To warn the council if it appears set on pursuing a course of action which is likely to be unlawful.

❏ If necessary, to ask the council to clarify a decision, so that it can be properly recorded in the minutes and properly implemented. For example, the clerk may need to intervene to ensure that the wording of a resolution is correctly noted.

❏ To express a point of view when asked to do so and when he feels it to be appropriate. This is sometimes a controversial point. Some councils discourage their clerk from expressing a point of view, presumably regarding the clerk is merely note-taker. However, the clerk is the chief – and usually the sole – executive officer and his views ought to be listened to by the council. (See further Chapter 4 "Qualifications, Training and Skills", below, page 87).

### 4. MINUTES

The minutes are intended to be a formal record of the acts and decisions of the council. They are not intended to be a record of the speeches of councillors. Accordingly, minutes should not normally include details of the reasons for decisions, nor of the discussions which precede the making of decisions, unless a decision cannot be expressed in any other way. The following are contrasting examples:

A. The council makes a decision by a recorded vote. The minutes should record the wording of the resolution

---

[28]  Para. 13(1) (England) and para. 29(1) (Wales) of Sch.12, LGA 1972.

containing the decision and whether or not the resolution was passed: e.g. "It was resolved by 9 votes to 5 that the clerk's salary be raised to £X with effect from 1st April 2000." (The reason for the decision is not recorded.)

B. The council discusses an issue without coming to a specific decision (a common occurrence). Here, the minutes should record the fact that the matter was discussed and the reason why no specific decision was made: e.g. "The Council received a proposal by Councillor Y to carry out a village appraisal and resolved to defer discussion of the matter to a special meeting to be held on [date]." (There was no recorded vote and the reason for the decision is recorded.)

There is no set format for the preparation of minutes. Nevertheless, the following points should be borne in mind by the clerk:

❑ The law requires that the minutes are recorded in a book kept for that purpose, or on separate pages in loose-leaf form, in which case the pages must be consecutively numbered and each page initialled when the minutes are signed.[29] This procedure is designed to prevent substitution of pages.

❑ The law also requires that the draft minutes of a meeting are signed (after being approved) at the same or the next suitable meeting of the council after the meeting in question (see page 8 above). The clerk should ensure that they are ready for signature.

❑ Consecutive numbering of items in the minutes is useful for reference and also as a guard against substitution or alteration.

---

[29] Para. 41(1) and (2) of Sch.12, LGA 1972.

❑ The names of the councillors present at a meeting must be recorded[30] and are almost invariably included in the minutes.

❑ Apologies for absence, *with reasons* (see page 7 above for the need to include reasons), should be recorded.

❑ Each minute, or group of minutes, should have a separate heading, which should normally be the heading of the relevant agenda item. There may be more than one decision recorded under a single heading. For example the heading "Finance" might have several items under it, such as accounts for payment, budget approval or setting of the precept.

❑ Minutes should be easy to read, with a neat layout. Decisions should be clearly identified. This can readily be achieved by the operative part of decisions being shown in bold or underlined type: e.g. "**It was resolved by 9 votes to 5** that the clerk's salary be raised to £X per year with effect from 1st April 2000."

❑ Where a resolution is subject to amendment, the minutes should record the original wording, any amendment or proposed amendment and the wording of the resolution as finally adopted: e.g. "It was moved by Councillor Y that the clerk's salary be raised to £5,000 a year with effect from 1st April 2000. An amendment to substitute '£5,500' for '£5,000' was moved by Councillor Z and was **lost by 9 votes to 5**. The original motion was then put to the vote and **it was resolved by 9 votes to 5** that the clerk's salary be raised to £5,000 a year with effect from 1st April 2000."

It is the responsibility of the clerk to prepare the minutes in draft form. It is not unknown for the clerk to be required

---

[30] Para. 40 of Sch.12, LGA 1972.

to submit the draft to the chairman for checking before distribution to other members of the council. Opinions vary as to the propriety of this procedure. The author's view is that the clerk should not submit the draft minutes to the chairman (or any other councillor) for checking. The clerk is the person at a meeting whose responsibility it is to take the notes on which the minutes are based. The chairman and other councillors cannot easily take notes as well as participating in debate and decision making. Furthermore, the clerk is (or ought to be) impartial, whereas a councillor, whether chairman or not, might be influenced by bias or personal feeling. The chairman and other councillors have the opportunity to correct errors (if any) in the draft minutes when these come before the council for approval.

Until the contrary is proved, a meeting of a council the minutes of which have been duly made and signed is deemed to have been duly convened and held, and all the members present are deemed to have been duly qualified.[31]

## 5. ADMINISTRATION

### Introduction

The work of the clerk entails a lot of paperwork and administration. He usually has no administrative assistance and works from home. He is left very much to his own devices in the organisation of the council's business and records. He therefore needs to devise, or adopt, management systems which enable him to run that business efficiently, effectively and economically (the "three Es", which the auditor is required to apply to the council's finances). If not already equipped with the appropriate skills, he should seek to acquire them, and it would normally be proper for the council to contribute the whole,

---

[31] Para. 41(3) of Sch.12, LGA 1972.

or some of, the cost of any training that is necessary. (See Chapter 4 "Qualifications, Training and Skills", below, page 87, for further advice.)

## Computers and associated equipment

It is likely that the majority of clerks now use a computer, rather than a typewriter or fountain pen, as the essential basic tool for administration of the council's affairs. Software programs are available which can provide administrative systems for a clerk, including programs for correspondence, agendas, minutes, budgets, accounts, reports, address lists, burial records, data storage and many other functions.

If the clerk has a computer, a printer will almost certainly be necessary as well, and possibly also a scanner. Access to the Internet and email (see below) requires a modem, which is now almost invariably built into the computer.

It is essential to ensure that all files and records on computer are regularly backed up on to disks. The frequency of back-up needs to be determined by the clerk. For a small council, a weekly back-up is probably sufficient. The back-up disks must be kept separate from the computer in a safe place (not in the same room). Failure to back up material could mean that irreplaceable records are lost in the event of the destruction of the computer or the corruption/loss of the information stored in it.

## Photocopiers

Most larger, and many medium sized and smaller, councils own or lease photocopiers. They are invaluable for producing sets of papers for council and other meetings, reports, etc. Some councils allow other organisations and individuals to use their copiers on a fee-paying basis – a welcome practice.

## Telephone, fax and email

Whilst correspondence is the normal method of formal communication between the clerk and others, no clerk could carry out his job properly without use of the telephone. Fax and email are also very frequently used. It may be worth having a separate line for fax and email so that the telephone can be used at the same time as these services. Communications by telephone may have to be confirmed in writing and copies of fax and email messages made for filing in the relevant files.

## The Internet and websites

Many clerks have access to the Internet and the vast array of information it contains, which can be of direct relevance to the work of local councils. An increasing number of local councils have their own websites or their own pages on someone else's website. These can be very useful, both to publicise the council's activities, etc. and also as sources of information and help to the clerks of other councils. The main local government associations, government departments and other organisations with which the council may come into contact all have their own websites; see Appendix 5 "Useful addresses and further reading" for details.

## Files and filing systems

It is the clerk's responsibility to organise the council's documentation, with the aim of:

— ensuring that essential and formal documents are retained and safely stored;

— establishing a filing system which stores "live" information in a form and place from which it can be easily retrieved;

— ensuring that "dead" information is regularly pruned from the council's files;

— ensuring that any legal requirements relating to the keeping of records are met;

— ensuring that those documents which are open to public inspection are readily available (if in the council's possession; old minute books, for example, may be deposited in the county record office).

It is common for the council to provide the clerk with the appropriate office equipment (e.g. computer or typewriter, printer, filing cabinet(s), fax machine, copier) or to pay the clerk an allowance for the use of the clerk's own office equipment. Similarly, the council should meet the cost of operating, maintaining, insuring and replacing the equipment and its peripherals (e.g. Internet and website subscription fees (if any), ink cartridges, disks, files and file folders).

(See Appendix 3 "Documents and Records" for guidance on the handling of council records.)

**Correspondence**

It is the clerk's responsibility to implement the council's decisions. This usually entails the writing of letters. These should be typed on the council's headed notepaper in proper business format. They should convey clearly the council's decision and should in general be impersonal in style. This does not mean that the recipient must always be addressed as "Sir" or "Madam", or as "Mr. X" or "Mrs. X". Letters can be addressed to persons by first name (if well known to the clerk) so long as the content is expressed with proper formality. A formal letter is in the public domain and may be seen not only by the recipient but also by others, including members of the council or of another local authority. (For example, the council's comments on a planning application will probably be seen by several of the local planning authority's staff and perhaps by members of its planning committee.)

The recipient of a well drafted, well presented letter is likely to look more favourably on the contents than if the letter is unclear and badly presented.

Copies should be kept of all letters despatched. These should normally be filed with related correspondence in the relevant file (see "Files and filing systems" above), although this may not be necessary if copies are kept on disk as part of a computer program.

It is generally inappropriate for the chairman or other councillors to write letters on behalf of the council, save for ceremonial or political reasons. For example, the chairman may properly invite other dignitaries to a civic ceremony or write a formal letter of complaint to the chairman of the district council on a policy issue.

Other administrative responsibilities of the clerk include: filing correspondence etc., keeping accounts (see page 31 below), and keeping secure the documents and records of the council (e.g. minute books, pecuniary interest books, electors' lists). Property documents such as title deeds, leases and licences are often deposited in a bank or with solicitors because the clerk does not have a safe or other secure storage facility.

Many councils have old documents and other records, often obtained by inheritance from authorities which they superseded when local councils were first established in 1894. Much of this material is likely to be of historical value and interest. For safety's sake, and to allow public access, a council would be wise to consider depositing such material in the local county record office on loan. (See Appendix 3 "Documents and Records".)

The clerk is often responsible for the preparation of publicity material issued by the council, such as press releases and parish newsletters. If so, this should be made clear in the clerk's job description and employment contract.

## 6. SUPERVISION OF STAFF

If the clerk is not the only employee of the council, it may be a requirement of the post to supervise and direct other staff (e.g. clerical assistants, grounds maintenance staff, caretakers).

As an employer, the council is subject to the enormous (and growing) mass of legislation governing the rights of employees, with which the clerk will need to have some familiarity.

The rights of employees are discussed in Chapter 3 "Employment Contract and Job Description" (page 51 below) in the context of the clerk's own employment. The advice given there applies equally to other council staff.

A particular responsibility of the clerk is to ensure that the Inland Revenue and Benefits Agency rules concerning the deduction of income tax and national insurance contributions (NIC) from the remuneration of employees is correctly carried out. Generally speaking, the deduction of tax is made under the PAYE (pay as you earn) system and is combined with the deduction of NIC. However, where an employee earns less than the PAYE threshold or the NIC threshold, deductions under the PAYE system are not usually made.

The Inland Revenue normally issues PAYE documentation to all employers. It contains useful advice on the PAYE system, including details of the PAYE and NIC thresholds.

Failure to deduct income tax and NIC under the PAYE system when under an obligation to do so can attract heavy penalties.

The extra responsibility entailed by the supervision of staff is normally recognised by an addition to the clerk's salary. SLCC and NALC jointly recommend a supplement linked to the number of staff supervised (see Chapter 3 "Employment and Job Description" page 64 below for details).

## 7. FINANCE

### Statutory requirements

The council is required to appoint an officer who is responsible for the administration of its financial affairs.[32] That person is almost always the clerk. It is the duty of the clerk, as responsible financial officer (RFO), to determine the form and content of the council's accounts and supporting records, subject to any directions from the council and in compliance with the Accounts and Audit Regulations 1996. The RFO must ensure that the accounts and records are maintained in accordance with proper practices and kept up to date.[33]

The RFO's accounting records must contain:[34]

---

[32] s. 151, LGA 1972.
[33] s. 2, ACA 1998 and Art. 4(1), AAR 1996.
[34] Art. 4(3), AAR 1996.

— details of the sums of money received and spent and the matters to which such sums relate;

— a record of the assets and liabilities of the council;

— a record of income and expenditure in relation to claims made, or to be made, for contribution, grant or subsidy from any Minister of the Crown.

The accounting control systems put in place by the RFO must include:[35]

— measures to ensure prompt and accurate recording of financial transactions, measures to prevent and detect inaccuracies and fraud and the ability to reconstitute any lost records;

— identification of the duties of officers dealing with financial transactions and division of responsibilities of those officers in relation to significant transactions;

— procedures for uncollectable amounts, including bad debts, not to be written off without the RFO's approval and for the approval to be shown in the accounting records.

The council must have an adequate and effective system of internal audit of its accounting records and control systems. The RFO must make available the relevant financial documents for the purposes of audit and supply the council with relevant information and explanation about such documents.[36]

The accounts must be made up to the 31st March in each year and must be prepared in compliance with the AAR

---

[35] Art. 4(4), AAR 1996.
[36] Art. 5, AAR 1996.

1996. These prescribe different requirements for different categories of council as follows[37] –

❏ Councils with a budgeted annual income in the relevant financial period and the previous two such periods of less than £5,000 must produce a receipts and payments account.

❏ Councils with a budgeted annual income in the relevant financial period and the two previous such periods of £5,000 or more but less than £500,000 must produce an income and expenditure account and a balance sheet.

❏ Councils with a budgeted annual income in the relevant financial period and the two previous such periods of £500,000 or more must produce a statement of accounts on the same basis as principal authorities. The main requirements are to prepare the following: an explanatory introduction; summarised statements of the income and expenditure of each fund for which separate accounts are kept; a summarised statement of capital expenditure; a statement of accounting policies; a consolidated revenue account; a consolidated balance sheet; a consolidated cash flow statement; notes to the accounts, including corresponding figures for the previous financial year.

Once the accounts have been prepared, the RFO must sign and date them and must certify that they present fairly the financial position of the council for the relevant accounting period. Once signed, dated and certified, the accounts must be approved by resolution of the council or of a relevant committee (e.g. a finance committee). The approval is to be given as soon as practicable after the period to which it

---

[37] Arts. 6 and 7, AAR 1996.

relates and in any event within six months after the end of the period.[38]

The approved accounts must be audited and publicised.[39]

## Investments

Any money which the council does not require for regular expenditure should be invested. The council does not have an unrestricted power of investment but can only invest in the securities authorised by the Trustee Investments Act 1961, as amended.

It is the clerk's responsibility to ensure that moneys are properly invested and that the necessary records are kept and preserved.

## General responsibilities

The statutory requirements outlined above place a lot of responsibility on the clerk as RFO. Detailed guidance on the preparation of budgets, accounts, audit and other financial matters is beyond the scope of this book. Reference should be made to a specialist work (see Appendix 7 "Further Reading" for some suggestions).

The council has to set a precept and a budget[40] and must approve all expenditure. It is the responsibility of the clerk, as RFO, to prepare the budget and, usually, to present the budget to the council. Medium sized and larger councils usually have a finance committee which is responsible for overseeing the budget process. In such cases, it is normally the task of the chairman of the committee to present the

---

[38] Art. 8, AAR 1996.
[39] Part II, ACA 1998; Arts. 9-17, AAR 1996.
[40] ss. 41 and 50, LGFA 1992.

budget to the council for approval, with the clerk providing assistance where necessary.

The council's precept must be set and issued to the billing authority (district or unitary council in England, county or county borough council in Wales) before 1st March in the financial year preceding that to which the precept relates.[41] The clerk therefore needs to ensure that the council's budget process is completed in good time for that date not to be missed.

All accounts and bills for payment must be properly authorised by the council or by a relevant functional committee. It is the clerk's responsibility to prepare lists of payments for authorisation at appropriate intervals and submit them to the council or committee.

Accounts should be settled promptly. If they are not, the council may incur interest charges for late payment, either under the terms of the contract or under statute.[42]

The clerk is responsible for drawing cheques and similar instruments. All cheques must be signed by two councillors.[43] It is a good practice for cheques to be signed at the meeting of the council or committee at which the relevant accounts for payment are authorised. It is also good practice for cheque counterfoils to be signed or initialled by the cheque signatory as a guard against fraud or falsification. Cheques should never be signed in blank.

The council is required to take security in relation to its officers who handle money or property.[44] This invariably takes the form of a fidelity guarantee insurance policy. The

---

[41]  s. 41, LGFA 1992.

[42]  Late Payment of Commercial Debts (Interest) Act 1998.

[43]  s. 150(5), LGA 1972.

[44]  s. 114, LGA 1972.

purpose of the policy is to cover the council against financial loss resulting from theft or misappropriation of council funds by the clerk and/or other officers of the council. The level of the cover should be a realistic estimate of the maximum amount the clerk might be able to misappropriate. The precise figure should be discussed with the council's insurer or broker.

## 8. MANAGEMENT OF LAND AND BUILDINGS

Most councils own or manage land or buildings, or both (e.g. allotments, cemeteries, parish halls, community centres, sports facilities). Unless the council employs staff specifically for property management purposes or uses professional managers (e.g. a firm of surveyors or estate agents), the general responsibility for management falls on the clerk. The management of land and buildings involves the following matters.

### A. Collection of rents and hiring charges

Where property is let on lease, it is desirable that the rent is paid by standing order into the council's bank account. This relieves the clerk of the need to check whether or not the rent has been paid on time and avoids the necessity for chasing up late payment or non-payment. Properties let on lease are likely to include:

— agricultural, commercial or residential property held by the council as an investment;

— recreational facilities, open spaces, halls and community centres often let to voluntary or charitable organisations.

Where premises or facilities are let or hired out for short periods (e.g. tennis courts, sports pitches, meeting rooms), the hire charges are normally paid by cheque or in cash and are collected in advance. The council should have a standard form of hire, setting out the terms and conditions of hire and the level of charges. Hire charges should be reviewed regularly, preferably at least once a year (most conveniently at the time the council's annual budget is prepared).

## B. Payment of rents and other charges

The clerk should ensure that rents and other payments due from the council are paid at the proper time.

## C. Maintenance and repair

Where property is let on lease, the terms of the lease will define the respective obligations of the council (as landlord) and the tenant with regard to maintenance and repair of the property. The clerk will need to be reasonably familiar with the terms of leases so as to be able to ensure that those obligations are properly carried out.

Whether let or not, council property should be properly maintained and repairs carried out promptly when necessary. Regular maintenance will reduce or eliminate the necessity for major repairs and thus save money. It may be appropriate for the council to establish repair and maintenance funds for all its properties or for individual properties.

Property insurance policies invariably require that the insured property is kept in a reasonable state of repair.

## D. Inspection of property

All council properties, buildings and structures, including open spaces, should be regularly inspected. There is a duty on the council to take reasonable steps to see that members of the public using its property are reasonably safe in so doing.[45] Performance of this duty necessarily involves regular inspections. Specialist inspections of some property may be necessary and should be entrusted to qualified experts. This is particularly so in the case of playground and sports equipment, which will usually require frequent visual inspection (often daily), apart from regular inspection at longer intervals by an expert (e.g. the NPFA – for address see Appendix 5).

## E. Insurance

It is essential that councils give full consideration to their insurance requirements at regular intervals – at least once a year, most conveniently when policies come up for renewal. If a council does not have adequate insurance, it could have to meet heavy claims from its own resources.

*Compulsory insurance*

Local councils are required by statute to take out three types of insurance: (1) employer's liability insurance, (2) fidelity guarantee insurance, and (3) motor vehicle insurance.

❑ *Employer's liability insurance:* a local council as employer must have insurance against liability for bodily injury or disease sustained by its employees, arising out of their employment.[46] It is an offence not to have this insurance, for which the maximum penalty on conviction is a fine of £2,500.[47]

❑ *Fidelity guarantee insurance:* section 114 of the LGA 1972 requires a local council to take such "security"

---

[45] Occupiers' Liability Acts 1957 and 1984.
[46] s. 1, Employers' Liability (Compulsory Insurance) Act 1969.
[47] s. 4, Employers' Liability (Compulsory Insurance) Act 1969.

(i.e. insurance) as it considers adequate against loss by reason of the acts (and omissions) of any employee who handles money or property. The amount of such insurance cover should be what the employee might be able to misappropriate, a figure which should be discussed with the council's insurer or broker.

❑ *Motor vehicle insurance:* if the council owns or leases motor vehicles, it must be covered against third party risks, as required by the Road Traffic Act 1988. In practice, comprehensive insurance will nearly always be required.

## Other types of insurance

Virtually no council will be properly insured if it relies only on the compulsory insurances. Other types of insurance will be necessary or desirable, depending on the scale and breadth of the council's responsibilities. These will include–

❑ *Public liability:* this will cover the council against its liabilities to members of the public. Such insurance is essential if the council owns, occupies or manages any land or property (e.g. playgrounds, village halls, community centres, offices, sports facilities, open spaces). It is designed to meet claims against the council for death, personal injury or damage to property (e.g. where a child is injured falling off an inadequately maintained swing). The minimum amount of cover should be £5 million.

❑ *Buildings and contents:* if the council owns or occupies buildings, it must in practice have adequate insurance against loss of or damage to the structure and contents. The amount of cover for buildings should be the full replacement cost (usually a requirement of the insurer), together with surveyors' and other fees, adjusted annually by reference to an appropriate price index (e.g. building costs). For contents, the insurance should cover replacement cost.

❑ *Structures, etc. in public places:* akin to contents insurance is insurance for street lights, place name and other signs, litter bins and similar street furniture and public structures. All these should be insured for the full replacement value.

❑ *Defamation:* councils, their members and their employees are occasionally threatened with, or subjected to, actions for defamation (libel or slander). Such actions can be very expensive to defend, even if unjustified, and insurance cover is sensible. Needless to say, councils, councillors and officers should always be careful in their public utterances to avoid defamatory expressions. An insurance policy will only protect against inadvertent defamation.

❑ *Accidents to members, voluntary assistants and employees:* a council may insure its members (and members of committees and sub-committees who are not councillors) and voluntary (unpaid) assistants against death and personal accident while on council business.[48] The council may also likewise insure its employees as part of their general conditions of service.[49]

❑ *Professional indemnity:* councils may insure against claims for loss resulting from professional negligence (e.g. giving negligent advice) on the part of the council, its members and employees.

❑ *Legal expenses:* some councils have legal expenses

---

[48] ss. 140 and 140A, LGA 1972.
[49] s. 112, LGA 1972.

insurance to cover themselves for the legal costs arising from the taking or defending of court action.

❑ *Events:* a large number of councils regularly organise celebratory events. Councils would be well advised to arrange special insurance against cancellation, delay, etc. as well as extending existing insurances where necessary (e.g. public liability).

### Insurance conditions and the avoidance of claims

It is invariable that insurers will require the council to take reasonable care to minimise the likelihood of claims, e.g. by keeping buildings, structures and other property in a safe condition and generally in good repair. This is particularly important where members of the public use council facilities or have access to council land. At common law and under occupier's liability and health and safety legislation, the council must ensure, as far as reasonably practicable, that the public can use its premises and facilities safely.[50] This, in turn, will normally involve regular, and often frequent, inspection so that damage is spotted and can be repaired quickly. Failure to take these precautions could lead to the insurer refusing to meet a claim.

Many insurers apply a condition to their property policies that the buildings, etc. must be insured for the full replacement cost. If that condition is not met, they will scale down claims and only pay a proportion of the loss (e.g. if replacement cost is £100,000 and insurance cover is £50,000, a claim will be scaled down by 50%). It is therefore essential that levels of cover are reviewed regularly, preferably annually. It is also sensible to review the general terms of insurance policies regularly to see that

---

[50] Occupiers' Liability Acts 1957 and 1984; Health and Safety at Work etc. Act 1974.

the council is covered against the risks which are relevant to its activities.

It is the clerk's responsibility to review the council's insurances and to make recommendations for any changes which appear necessary or desirable.

## F. Documentation

The clerk is normally responsible for the safety and security of title deeds, leases, licences, insurance policies and other documents relating to the ownership and management of property. Unless the clerk has a safe or similar secure storage facilities, title deeds and the like should be lodged in a bank or with the council's solicitors. The clerk would be well advised to keep a list or register of the council's property holdings.

Appendix 3 "Documents and Records" contains detailed advice about documents and records.

## 9. MANAGEMENT OF GOODS AND CHATTELS

Most councils own a miscellany of goods and chattels, of which the following are examples:

— office equipment, including computers, printers, scanners, copiers, telephones, fax machines, filing cabinets and stationery supplies;

— minute books, account books, books and papers relating to council activities both past and present (see Appendix 3 "Documents and Records" for details);

— playground equipment, including swings, skateboard ramps, slides and roundabouts;

— grounds maintenance equipment, including mowers, gardening implements and line markers;

— sports equipment (both indoor and outdoor), including goal posts and nets and gym equipment;

— furniture (both indoor and outdoor), including chairs and tables, benches, notice boards, street lamps, public clocks, shelters, flag poles, litter bins and fencing;

— ceremonial and historic property, including maces, regalia, robes and charters.

Proper records must be kept of all movable property and adequate insurance cover must be maintained. Equipment in regular use must be inspected frequently and repaired or replaced as necessary.

## 10. THE CLERK'S RELATIONSHIP WITH COUNCILLORS AND OTHERS

A successful local council depends for its success on the councillors and the clerk playing complementary roles to ensure that the council devises appropriate policies and the clerk carries them out. This is particularly so where, as in most cases, the clerk is the only employee of the council and is, in effect, its chief executive.

It is therefore important that the clerk and the councillors understand each other's role and that they work closely and harmoniously together. This is especially relevant in relation to the respective roles of the clerk and the chairman. Without each party fully understanding their own role and the role of the other, disagreements and misunderstandings may arise.

### The role of the councillor

As a general rule, the role of a councillor is likely to involve the following:

❏ The management of a small, medium or large enterprise, depending upon the resources available to the council and its level of activity. This in turn will involve one or more of the following –

- Fixing a budget. There is a statutory requirement for all councils to prepare an annual budget and it is in practice impossible to plan ahead without doing so. The responsibility for preparing the budget rests primarily on the clerk or financial officer (usually the same person), but the council must approve the final version. Most policy decisions of the council have, or may have, financial implications and these need to be considered at the same time as the policy.

- Making management policy decisions. These are usually made by the council itself but, in medium and large councils, some decision making is delegated to committees.

- Issuing guidance to and controlling staff (in small and medium councils usually part time). Since most councils have only one part time employee – the clerk – it is very important that the council ensures that, as far as possible, a suitable person is appointed to the post. This in turn requires an understanding and appreciation of the position of the clerk.

- Checking that decisions taken by the council (and its committees, if any) are properly implemented. The responsibility for policy implementation rests primarily with the clerk; the council makes the decisions and the clerk carries them out. However, particularly in smaller councils, councillors often have a role to play in policy implementation, for example in the representation of the views of the council or the community to others (e.g. as a spokesman for the council at meetings with other bodies such as district councils or as a council appointee on the committee of a local voluntary organisation).

❑ To suggest new initiatives or developments of existing policies. For example, many councils have undertaken village appraisals, in order to discover what local people want for their community, as a first step towards new policies. A village appraisal should seek to involve the whole community, with councillors taking a leading role.

❑ To ensure that the views of the community are put to the relevant persons or bodies and that the special interests of the community are protected or promoted.

## The role of the chairman

As well as the foregoing, the chairman has a special position as the elected head of the council. The chairman must preside at council meetings (unless absent) and is responsible for seeing that meetings are conducted properly, with the aim of producing intelligible decisions. He also has to represent the council to the local community and the local community to others.

## The relationship between the clerk and councillors

As indicated in the introduction above, the smooth running of the council and its affairs depends upon a harmonious and positive relationship between the clerk and the councillors. It is essential that each party understands the role of the other and that, as far as possible, their respective roles do not overlap. It is thus incorrect in principle for a councillor to undertake administrative tasks which are properly those of the clerk (e.g. writing letters on behalf of the council) except in an emergency, and only then with the authority of the council. In the same way, it is incorrect for the clerk to usurp the role of councillors by, for example, seeking to impose his views on policy issues on the council. The clerk should not forget that he is the employee of the council and that the councillors may sometimes make decisions with which he does not agree.

Any personal relationship between the clerk and a councillor (e.g. father and son, husband and wife) should not be allowed to influence the conduct of the council's affairs.

It is not unknown for animosity to exist between a councillor and the clerk. This can arise because of the failure of the councillor in question to understand that the clerk's loyalty and responsibility is to the council as a whole and not to individual councillors. Such a situation can arise, for example, where a councillor wishes to be provided with information by the clerk in order to further a personal matter in which the council is not involved. A clerk should resist any request of this nature and should, if necessary, obtain the support of the council.

## The relationship between the clerk and the chairman

As a councillor, the chairman of the council should have regard to the clerk/councillor relationship considerations dealt with above. In addition, the special position of the chairman means that his relationship with the clerk is also special.

Examples of this special relationship are –

❑ It is common practice for the clerk and the chairman to discuss the contents of a draft agenda for a meeting before it is finalised. Once the agenda has been sent out, it is again common practice for the chairman and the clerk to go through the agenda before the meeting. This can help the chairman ensure that the agenda items are properly discussed at the meeting. It can also help the clerk to prepare any necessary advice or guidance for councillors on agenda items.

❑ If the clerk has a grievance, it is usual for the chairman to be the first person with whom the clerk raises the matter.

❑ If a disciplinary issue arises, the chairman is usually the person who takes the matter up with the clerk.

The complaint is sometimes heard that the chairman and the clerk "run the council". Although the chairman and the clerk frequently have a special relationship, they must not (consciously or otherwise) seek to control the council or to arrogate to themselves the council's decision-making responsibilities.

Anecdotal evidence suggests that there is a large annual turnover of clerks. Regrettably, a significant proportion of the turnover probably results from the resignation or dismissal of clerks because of a failure to establish a proper working relationship with their councils or chairmen. This should not occur if councils and clerks take heed of the advice given above.

## The clerk's relationships with other people

As the council's chief executive, the clerk will come into contact with persons from all walks of life. The first, often informal, contact and communication between the clerk and the people with whom he regularly deals is invaluable. The establishment of a personal rapport with such people will make the task of a clerk considerably easier. This is particularly true in the case of officials of other local authorities, agencies and organisations with which the council has regular contact. A telephone call to the local area manager of the highway authority is more likely to secure the speedy unblocking of a road drain than writing a formal letter to the County Surveyor.

In addition, an ability to deal with members of the public is highly desirable. A number of local councils are now providing a "one stop shop" where information and advice about local services and facilities (including those of the other local authorities serving the area and, sometimes, other organisations) is available.

The clerk may receive complaints about the activities of the council or of individual councillors. These need to be handled sensitively and positively. The council ought to have a formal procedure for dealing with complaints, details of which can be given to those who wish to complain. Since local councils are not subject to the jurisdiction of the Commissioner for Local Administration (the Local Ombudsman), there is no independent body to adjudicate on complaints against them (but under the Local Government Act 2000, the conduct of councillors will be subject to scrutiny by independent Standards Boards – see Appendix 8).

It is common, too, for the clerk to receive complaints about the services, etc. (or lack of them) provided by other local authorities. The complainants should be advised of the appropriate authority and department to contact. It may also be advisable to make informal contact with the relevant officer of the authority to warn that a complaint may be on its way – another case where the value of a personal rapport with officers of another authority is clearly shown.

(For advice about the skills and personal qualities which clerks may need, see Chapter 4 "Qualifications, Training and Skills" below, page 87).

## 11. INITIATIVES AND GUIDANCE

Depending upon the role of the council, the clerk may be expected to show initiative and be prepared to offer guidance to the council on matters of policy as well as administration.

The clerk should consider exercising initiative by suggesting courses of action for the council to discuss, reviewing the progress of the council's policies and, if necessary, suggesting changes. However, the clerk must never forget that the council decides policy matters and is always free to turn down suggestions made by the clerk.

The clerk should be in a good position to advise and guide the council on the adoption and implementation of policies. As the council's chief (or only) executive officer, he will have, or have access to, a great deal of information relevant to the council's powers and functions; such information can and should be used to assist the council in setting its policies.

# CHAPTER 3

# EMPLOYMENT CONTRACT AND JOB DESCRIPTION

## *INTRODUCTION*

A council has a duty to appoint such officers as are necessary for the proper discharge of its functions. An officer so appointed holds office on such reasonable terms and conditions, including conditions relating to remuneration, as the council thinks fit.[51] The duty is subject to the general power of local authorities to do anything which is calculated to facilitate, or is conducive or incidental to, the discharge of any of their functions.[52]

The council also has a power to appoint one or more councillors as officers, without remuneration.[53] (For more detailed advice on this point, see Chapter 5 "The Role of Local Councils", below, page 105).

Every appointment to a paid office made by a local council must be made on merit,[54] but subject to:

❏ Section 7 of the Sex Discrimination Act 1975 (discrimination permitted in relation to employment where the sex of an employee is a genuine occupational qualification).

❏ Section 5 of the Race Relations Act 1976 (discrimination permitted in relation to employment where being of a particular group is a genuine occupational qualification).

---

[51] s. 112(1) and (2), LGA 1972.
[52] s. 111, LGA 1972.
[53] s. 112(3), LGA 1972.
[54] s. 7, LGHA 1989.

❑ Sections 5 and 6 of the Disability Discrimination Act 1995 (defining discrimination and requiring employers to make adjustments to workplaces to accommodate disabled people).

Sections 5 and 6 of the 1995 Act do not apply in relation to an employer who has fewer than 20 employees.

Whilst the council may appear to have a very wide discretion in relation to the terms on which officers are engaged, that discretion is fettered in many ways by the common law and legislation covering the employment of staff.

### EMPLOYED OR SELF-EMPLOYED?

The legislation referred to above does not specify the legal relationship between a council and its officers. At least in theory (as to practice, see below, page 53), they can be appointed either on an employed basis or on a self-employed basis. It is therefore important to draw a distinction between employment and self-employment.

There is no simple and definitive method of deciding whether a person is employed or self-employed. A number of factors are relevant, of which the following are examples: the extent of the employer's control over the work done by the employee; the regularity of hours worked, the presence or absence of provisions relating to holidays and sickness, the arrangements for the payment of income tax and national insurance contributions; the method of terminating the contract of engagement; whether or not the employee bears the risk of loss and enjoys the opportunity for profit; whether or not the employee is the holder of an office. Perhaps the most important factor is that relating to profit and loss because this will often determine whether or not a person is in business on his own account, or is working for someone else.

The distinction between employment and self-employment can be very important. As a general rule, the voluminous legislation which covers employment rights and obligations does not apply to the self-employed. Similarly, the remuneration of a self-employed person is taxed differently from that of an employee and the payment of social security contributions is handled differently. The obligations of an employer to an employee are more onerous than those of a person who contracts services from a self-employed person.

The clerk of a council is almost invariably an employee because the terms of engagement are such that he is not in business on his own account so far as the clerkship is concerned. Should there be any doubt about the matter, a council and its clerk would be well advised to ensure that the clerk is an employee rather than self-employed. The council will be able to exercise proper control over the clerk's work and the clerk will be covered by the employment legislation.

## THE LEGAL POSITION OF THE CLERK

The clerk is the chief executive officer of the council and often its only paid employee. He is, as well, in almost all cases the proper officer of the council. As indicated immediately above, the clerk is almost invariably an employee of the council and it will be assumed for the purposes of the advice given in this book that the clerk is an employee.

### The proper officer

There are numerous references to the "proper officer" of a local authority in legislation (e.g. the person to receive declarations of acceptance of office under section 83 of the Local Government Act 1972 and to receive copies of byelaws made by a district or unitary council under section 236 of the same Act). That person is the officer appointed by the council to perform the functions of the proper officer.[55] For the avoidance of doubt, the council should normally specify the clerk as its proper officer. This can be done in the clerk's employment contract. Many councils also, or alternatively, make provision in a standing order for the clerk to be the proper officer of the council.

## The legal relationship between the clerk and the council

The legal relationship between clerk and council is primarily contractual. This means that the two parties enter into a legally binding agreement or contract when the council engages the clerk as its employee. Perhaps rather oddly, despite the huge mass of employment legislation, there is no legal requirement that the contract must be in writing. However, statute requires that every employee is provided with a statement of particulars of employment within two months after the start of the employment.[56] These particulars can be incorporated in a contract of employment so that the contract complies with the statutory provisions. The particulars which must be included in the statutory statement are set out in the legislation, but the contract may include other matters.

It cannot be too strongly urged that there should be a written contract of employment between council and clerk. It is convenient if the contract includes the statutory particulars so that all the clerk's terms of employment are in one document.

Employment legislation confers rights and obligations on both employers and employees. The legislation is normally

---

[55] s. 270(1), LGA 1972.
[56] s. 1, ERA 1996.

binding and cannot be avoided by contractual provisions in a contract of employment. These matters do not normally appear in such a contract unless some variation from the statutory provisions is permitted. A summary of the main statutory provisions is set out below.

## The obligations of the clerk

Apart from legislation, there is a general obligation under the ordinary law on an employee to serve his employer faithfully during the course of his employment. He must not, for example, make secret profits out of his employment, a matter which is partly covered by legislation.[57] This requires any officer employed by a local authority to disclose any pecuniary interest, direct or indirect, in a contract which the authority has entered into, or proposes to enter into (other than a contract to which the officer is a party).

Under the same legislation,[58] a clerk must not accept any fee or reward for his employment other than his proper remuneration.

## The terms of the clerk's contract of employment

Subject to the foregoing, the terms of the contract are largely as agreed between the parties. However, certain matters must, in practice, normally be included and these are set out in the next section. Those required to be included in the statutory statement of particulars are marked "SP".

## Standard contractual terms

*The names and addresses of the council and the clerk (SP)*

This is self-explanatory.

---

[57] s. 117(1), LGA 1972.
[58] s. 177(2), LGA 1972.

## Commencement of employment (SP)

The date on which the employment began should be stated, which would not necessarily be the date of the contract.

## Period of continuous employment (SP)

The date on which the clerk's period of continuous employment began, taking into account any employment with a previous employer which counts towards that period, should be stated. This date can be important, because an employee enjoys certain statutory rights only if his employment has been continuous for a particular minimum period (e.g. the right not to be unfairly dismissed applies only if the period of continuous employment is not less than one year).[59] As a general rule, continuous employment relates to employment by one employer, but in some cases legislation provides that a period of employment with a previous employer is included in the period of continuous employment.[60] Otherwise, the clerk and the council can agree that a period of employment by a previous employer or previous employers can be included in the clerk's period of continuous employment. It is normal for previous and contemporaneous employment in the local government service (including service as a local council clerk or other local council employee) to be so included. A number of clerks, for example, are full-time employees of principal local authorities as well as being clerks of local councils.

## Fixed-term employment (SP)

If the clerk's job is not intended to be permanent (an unusual situation), the statutory statement should contain particulars of the period for which the job is to last or the date on which it is to terminate.

---

[59] s. 108, ERA 1996 and Unfair Dismissal and Statement of Reasons for Dismissal (Variation of Qualifying Period) Order 1999 (S.I. 1999 No. 277).
[60] s. 218, ERA 1996.

## The legal position of the clerk

### Job title (SP)

The job title will usually need be no more than a statement that the clerk is employed as clerk to X parish, community or town council and that the clerk will be the proper officer of the council.

### Job description (SP)

The statutory statement of particulars may contain a brief job description instead of a job title. A full job description will set out in some detail the work the clerk is contracted to undertake. It is often convenient for the job description to be a separate document and this will almost certainly be the case where the job description has been issued to applicants for a vacant clerkship. If the job description is in a separate document, that document should be incorporated into the contract by reference. A specimen job description can be found in Appendix 2. The council may reserve the right to vary the duties of the clerk, and amend the job description, if circumstances so require.

### Salary (SP)

Details should be given of:

— the gross salary;

— the intervals at which the salary is paid (weekly, monthly, etc.);

— the salary scale (if any);

— how the salary is paid (by cheque, direct to the clerk's bank account, etc.);

— any additional payments for supervising staff, etc. (see below, page 64).

All workers (including local council clerks) are covered by

the National Minimum Wage Act 1998 and the National Minimum Wage Regulations 2000 (S.I. 2000 No. 1114). These enactments prescribe a minimum wage for workers aged 18 to 21 of £3.20 per hour and for adult workers £3.70 per hour.

SLCC and NALC make joint recommendations for minimum salaries for both full-time and part-time clerks. The basic recommendations are that –

(a) a full-time clerk should be paid in accordance with the LC scale, which is derived from the salary scale for administrative and similar staff employed by principal authorities issued by the NJC; and

(b) a part-time clerk should be paid at an hourly rate derived from the LC scale.

The LC scale is as follows –

| Scale and Population | | Spinal Column Points |
|---|---|---|
| LC1 | Up to 5,000 | 15 – 21 |
| LC2 | 5,001 – 10,000 | 22 – 27 |
| LC3 | 10,001 – 15,000 | 28 – 33 |
| LC4 | 15,001 – 20,000 | 34 – 39 |
| LC5 | 20,001 – 25,000 | 40 – 45 |
| LC6 | 25,001 – 30,000 | 46 – 51 |
| LC7 | Over 30,000 | 52 – 57 |

The actual salary levels payable in accordance with the above scales are those which are agreed between the principal local authority employers and trade unions represented on the NJC on an annual basis and are adopted by SLCC and NALC. The annual NJC settlement date is 1st April (the start of the local government year).

The appropriate spinal column point (SPC) for a starting salary will depend on the ability and experience of the newly appointed clerk. The clerk's salary should rise annually by one SPC until the top of the relevant LC scale is reached. This means that, while a clerk's salary is progressing up a scale, he will receive two pay increases each year; one being the increment from one SPC to the next and the other being the national annual pay award set by the NJC. Once the clerk's salary reaches the top of the scale, further increases in salary will usually be limited to the national pay award, unless there is a change of circumstances, such as an additional payment for supervising staff or in recognition of examination success (see below).

The LC salary scale is adapted for part-time clerks by reference to the hourly rate of pay earned in the standard local government working week of 37 hours. Thus a clerk who works 20 hours per week for a council where the population of the parish/community is under 5,000 and whose salary is on SCP15 should receive a minimum weekly salary calculated as the following example shows –

SCP 15 for 1999/2000 = £12,081 or £232.33 per week
Hourly rate is £232.33/37 = £6.28
Minimum weekly salary is £6.28 x 20 = £125.60

A council which pays the clerk at least the recommended scale salary will comply with the National Minimum Wage Act 1998 and the Regulations made under it. However, a council is not obliged to use the LC Scale, so long as the remuneration paid to the clerk (and other employees, if any) is reasonable.

SLCC and NALC also recommend that clerks of parish and town councils within the London fringe areas are paid the

London Fringe Area allowance, which is part of the NJC's general conditions of service. The allowance is intended to compensate employees for the higher cost of living in the London fringe areas than elsewhere.

The clerk is entitled to be provided with a written **itemised pay statement** at or before the time when his salary is paid.[61] The statement must contain:

— the gross amount of the salary;

— the amounts of any variable and, normally, fixed deductions from the gross amount and the purposes for which they are made (e.g. national insurance and pension contributions);

— the net amount of the salary;

— where different parts of the net amount are paid in different ways, the amount and method of each part-payment.

Separate detailed provision is made in the legislation for a standing statement of fixed deductions to be given instead of those deductions being part of the ordinary pay statement.[62]

*Hours of work (SP)*
For full-time clerks, the normal hours of work will usually be similar to those applicable to other full-time jobs in local government. The NJC conditions of service provide for a standard 37-hour working week. For most part-time clerks, it may not be practicable to specify the hours of work. They usually work on their own from home and cannot confine their working time to fixed hours. However, if the clerk's

---

[61]  s. 8, ERA 1996.
[62]  s. 9, ERA 1996.

salary is calculated in accordance with the recommended formula (see above), the number of hours to be worked in each relevant period (week, month, quarter or year) should be stated. Whether the clerk is full or part-time, provision should be made for attendance at council and committee meetings and at the annual parish or town meeting in the evenings, or otherwise outside standard working hours.

Under the Working Time Regulations 1998 (S.I. 1998 No. 1833), there are restrictions on the number of hours per week worked by employees. The basic rule is that a worker cannot be required to work more than an average of 48 hours per week. However, this limit does not apply where (to quote from the Regulations) "... on account of the specific characteristics of the activity in which he is engaged, the duration of his working time is not measured or predetermined or can be determined by the worker himself ..." Most local council clerks, being part-time and working from home, come within this classification because they have control over the hours they work and their work time is not monitored or determined by their employer. As indicated above, the number of hours the clerk is expected to work (and to be paid for) can be included in the statutory particulars and the contract of employment.

### Place of work (SP)

A full-time clerk will normally work from an office provided by the council and, if so, this should be the specified place of work. As indicated above, most part-time clerks work from home, in which case this should usually be specified as the place of work. Sometimes, the clerk is required to attend at a specified location for a stated number of hours each week (e.g. at the village hall on each weekday between 10 am and 12 noon). This, too, should be included in the contract.

## Holidays and holiday pay (SP)

An employee with at least 13 weeks' service has a statutory right to a minimum period of paid holiday each year. The amount is currently four weeks (as from 23rd November 1999).[63] A week's leave is equivalent to the time the employee would work during a week. Thus an employee working a five-day week would be entitled to 20 days' paid leave a year. Where the employee works irregular hours or works part-time, he has the right to a proportionate amount of the annual leave which a full-time employee would have. Thus a part-time employee working the equivalent of two days a week would be entitled to two-fifths of the entitlement of a full-time employee working five days a week (i.e. 8 days). Public and Bank Holidays are included in the statutory four-week period, although it is common for these days to be allowed as additional days of paid leave (as in the NJC conditions of service). A statutory procedure is set out for employers and employees to inform each other when leave is, and is not, to be taken. Alternatively, they can make an agreement about these matters.

The statutory statement must also contains details of an employee's entitlement to accrued holiday pay on termination of employment.

It is open to employers and employees to agree terms for holidays and holiday pay which are more generous than the statutory minimum (see the section "General conditions of employment", below, page 68).

Whether the council and clerk rely on the statutory provisions or make specific arrangements for holidays, it may not always be easy to make provision for holidays for part-time clerks. They usually work irregular hours and

---

[63] Working Time Regulations 1998 (S.I. 1998 No. 1833).

have no deputy or substitute to take over when they are on leave. It may well be better, therefore, not simply to rely on the statutory provisions.

### Absence from work through sickness or injury (SP)

Provision is usually made for the clerk to be entitled to his salary for a specified number of days during a year when absent through sickness or injury, less any statutory sick pay or other social security payments received. There may also be provisions requiring the clerk to produce a doctor's certificate if the period of absence through illness exceeds a specified number of days.

The legislation on statutory sick pay is lengthy and complicated and is outside the scope of this book. It is sufficient to note the following:

— an employee is not entitled to statutory sick pay if his salary is less than the lower earnings limit for national insurance purposes. Many part-time clerks come into this category;

— contractual payments of salary during periods of incapacity for work are set against statutory sick pay. Thus an employer who makes such payments at a rate higher than statutory sick pay is relieved of the obligation to pay SSP.

### Pension and pension schemes (SP)

All principal local authorities are members of the Local Government Pension Scheme (LGPS)[64] and their employees are normally entitled to join the Scheme. Local councils are not members of the Scheme unless they resolve to

---

[64] Local Government Pension Scheme Regulations 1997 (S.I. 1997 No. 1612), as amended.

become members. It is usually appropriate for a full-time or nearly full-time clerk to join a contributory pension scheme and, if so, the employing council should become a member of the LGPS. Full details of the Scheme can be obtained from the appropriate administering authority. Perhaps rather strangely, the statutory statement of particulars does not have to contain details of pension arrangements made under a pension scheme established by or under statute (as the LGPS is).[65]

Pension arrangements for part-time clerks vary. Some join the LGPS, some are members of another pension scheme by virtue of other paid employment, some make individual provision through a personal pension plan and some have no pension arrangements at all. If no pension is provided, the council has a discretionary power to pay a gratuity to an employee on retirement or to the spouse and dependants of an employee who dies in service.[66]

If there are no pension arrangements for the clerk, the contract should say so.

For more detailed information about pensions and gratuities see "Pensions and gratuities" on page 78 below.

### Supervision of staff

If the clerk is not the only employee, it may be a requirement of the post to supervise other staff (e.g. clerical staff, grounds maintenance staff, caretakers). SLCC and NALC recommend that the council pays a supplement to the clerk's salary to reflect the additional responsibility. The amount of the supplement depends on the number of staff, in accordance with the following bands: 2-5, 6-10, 11-20,

---

[65] s. 1(5), ERA 1996.

[66] Local Government (Discretionary Payments) Regulations 1996 (S.I. 1996 No. 1680), as amended.

21-30, 31-40, 41-50, 51-60, 61-70, over 70. (For more advice on the supervision of staff see Chapter 2 "The Role of the Clerk", page 30 above).

## Recognition of qualifications

SLCC and NALC recommend that a clerk who obtains a relevant qualification should be paid extra by having their salary increased by one SPC for each level of qualification. The recommendation applies to the courses in Local Policy offered by the Cheltenham and Gloucester College of Higher Education and is as follows:

*Certificate of Higher Education*
   1st year – one increment

*Certificate of Higher Education*
   Completion of Level I – two increments

*Diploma of Higher Education*
   Completion of Level II – three increments

*Bachelor of Arts (Hons.)*
   Completion of Level III – four increments.

SLCC and NALC also recommend that a council should consider giving increments to a clerk who obtains other relevant qualifications.

## Grievance procedure

It is very important that the contract includes clear provisions to deal with any grievances of the clerk relating to his employment. A significant number of clerks resign because they are unable to obtain a satisfactory solution to genuine grievances. It is usually appropriate for the contract to provide for the clerk initially to seek informal resolution of a grievance by approaching the chairman. If this does not resolve the matter, or if a formal procedure is in any event desired, the grievance should be put in writing and referred to the council or to a relevant committee. When the grievance is discussed, the clerk should be given a chance to make oral representations, either in person or through a representative.

The decision of the council or committee is usually final. If the clerk is still dissatisfied, he may have to consider resignation. If the council has failed to deal properly, or at all, with a genuine grievance, the clerk may have no alternative but to resign. Resignation in such circumstances could amount to constructive dismissal, which would entitle the clerk to seek compensation, or even reinstatement, from an Employment Tribunal.

All "workers" (which includes all employees) have a statutory right to be represented at a grievance or a disciplinary hearing by a trade union officer or a fellow worker.[67]

## Disciplinary procedure

It is also very important for the contract to include clear provisions covering disciplinary action against the clerk. Normally, there should be a requirement that the clerk is informed in writing of the nature of any breach of rules of conduct or otherwise unacceptable behaviour and is given an opportunity to answer at a meeting of the council or an appropriate committee. If such a procedure is adopted, the contract will have to specify rules of conduct and what constitutes unacceptable behaviour. The contract will also have to specify the sanctions which apply if a breach of rules of conduct or unacceptable behaviour is found. A common provision is for gross misconduct to result in instant dismissal and for lesser misconduct to be subject

---

[67] s. 10, ERA 1999.

to a system of warnings. If the warnings are ignored, the clerk may be dismissed. If a clerk is dismissed in breach of a disciplinary procedure, the dismissal may be unfair and, again, the clerk may seek a remedy from an Employment Tribunal.

ACAS (for address, see Appendix 5 below, page 130) has issued a Code of Practice on Disciplinary and Grievance Procedures which contains useful guidance on these matters.

*Termination (SP)*

The statutory statement of particulars must contain details of the length of notice the employee is obliged to give and entitled to receive to terminate his or her contract. The minimum period of notice which an employer must give an employee who has been continuously employed for a month or more is as follows:[68]

— where the employee has been employed for less than two years, one week;

— where the employee has been employed for two years or more but less than twelve years, one week's notice for each year of continuous employment;

— where the employee has been employed for twelve years or more, twelve weeks.

An employee who has been continuously employed for one month or more must give his employer at least one week's notice of termination.[69]

The foregoing are minimum periods of notice and they override any contractual notice periods which are shorter.

---

[68] s. 86(1), ERA 1996.
[69] s. 86(2), ERA 1996.

However, the council and the clerk may agree on longer periods. The normal practice is to provide that either party shall give a stated minimum period of written notice to the other to end the contract.

## General conditions of employment (SP)

The statutory statement of particulars must include details of any collective agreements which directly affect the terms and conditions of employment including, where the employer is not a party, the persons by whom they were made.

The NJC has promulgated general Conditions of Service for full-time administrative, etc. employees in local government. These are a form of collective agreement. The Conditions can be adopted by local councils, either wholly or with modifications. The Conditions make provision, for example, for holidays and holiday pay, the reimbursement of expenses and the payment of allowances, as well as for regular revisions of salary scales.

## Maternity benefits, parental and dependants' leave

Employees are generally entitled to maternal leave, parental leave and leave to look after dependants.[70] The statutory provisions are lengthy and complicated. Only a summary of them is set out here.

*Maternity benefits:* Female employees are entitled to time off for antenatal care, maternity leave, maternity benefit and protection against unfair treatment or dismissal:

❑ *Time off for antenatal care:* female employees are entitled to time off to keep appointments for antenatal care made

---

[70] Part VIII, ERA 1996 as substituted by Sch. 4, Employment Relations Act 1999.

on the advice of a doctor, midwife or health visitor. If required, the employee must show the employer a certificate from the doctor, etc. confirming that she is pregnant and an appointment card or other evidence showing that an appointment has been made. An employee should normally be paid during the time off at her normal rate of pay.

❏ *Maternity leave:* a pregnant employee is entitled to at least 18 weeks' ordinary maternity leave. During this period, her contract of employment continues in force and she is entitled to receive all her contractual benefits except wages or salary.

❏ *Additional maternity leave:* a female employee who has completed one year's continuous employment with her employer is entitled to additional maternity leave. This runs from the end of the ordinary maternity leave until the end of the 29th week, beginning with the week in which the baby is born.

❏ *Maternity benefit:* a pregnant employee is entitled to **statutory maternity pay** if she has worked for her employer for at least 26 weeks and her wages or salary are at least equal to the lower earnings limit for national insurance contributions. The rate of statutory maternity pay is 90% of the employee's average weekly earnings for the first six weeks of leave and thereafter at a flat rate. If not entitled to statutory maternity pay, a pregnant employee may be able to claim **maternity allowance**. This is available to women who have been employed or self-employed and have paid national insurance contributions in 26 out of the 66 weeks ending with the week before the expected childbirth. The maximum period for which maternity allowance can be claimed is 18 weeks. Maternity allowance is paid at a flat rate. Women expecting babies after 20th August 2000 who do not qualify for SMP and who are earning at least £30 per week will qualify for maternity allowance.

Many part-time clerks will not be entitled either to statutory maternity pay or maternity allowance because they do not earn enough.

❑ *Protection against unfair treatment or dismissal:* generally speaking, a female employee who takes maternity leave is entitled to return to her employment after the period of leave has ended on the same terms and conditions as before. An employee who is dismissed during ordinary or additional maternity leave, at the end of leave or after resuming work, by reason of the fact that she has taken maternity leave, is entitled to claim for unfair dismissal through an Employment Tribunal.

*Parental leave:* This is a new right to take time off work to look after a child or make arrangements for the child's welfare. The right applies to full-time and part-time employees, provided that they have been employed for at least 12 months. It does not apply to self-employed persons. The main provisions relating to the right are as follows:

— it applies up the child's fifth birthday, or for five years after adoption (up to the age of 18), or up to the child's 18th birthday if the child is disabled;

— it is enjoyed by both mothers and fathers, natural and adoptive, provided that the child or children were born, or were adopted, after 14th December 1999 (the date on which the relevant legislation was brought into force);

— each parent can take a total of 13 weeks' leave for each child. This cannot be taken all at once (unless the employer agrees). If there is no agreement between employer and employee, the leave must be taken in blocks of one week or more, up to a maximum of 4 weeks per year for each child;

— unless otherwise agreed, at least 21 days' notice must be given of the intention to take parental leave;

— there is no statutory right to be paid during parental leave: it is a matter for agreement between employer and employee;

— employees are protected from detriment in their employment and against dismissal for exercising their right to parental leave.

*Dependants' leave:* This is another new right for employees, in force from 15th December 1999. The main provisions relating to the right are as follows:

— the right apples to all employees, both full and part-time;

— the nature of the right is to have time off from work to deal with a sudden or unexpected problem concerning a dependant (e.g. illness, injury, having a baby, making longer term care arrangements for a dependant who is ill or injured, death, unexpected accident to a child during school hours);

— a dependant is a husband, wife, child, parent, or someone living in the same household as the employee (such as an elderly grandparent). A tenant, lodger or living-in employee does not count as a dependant;

— the employee is entitled to a reasonable amount of time off, according to the nature of the emergency;

— there is no statutory limit on the number of times leave can be taken;

— employees are protected from detriment and dismissal in the same way as those who take parental leave.

## EXPENSES AND ALLOWANCES

### Expenses

The clerk inevitably incurs expenses in carrying out the duties of office. He is entitled to be reimbursed by the council for such expenses because he incurs them on behalf of the council. Examples are: the purchase of stationery and postage stamps, telephone/fax/email calls, travelling expenses in attending meetings or other events on behalf of, or as a representative of, the council.

The council has an inherent power to pay the expenses of the clerk and other officers.[71]

The method of reimbursement is a matter for agreement between the council and the clerk. One method is for the clerk to submit a statement of expenses incurred for payment at the same time as his salary; this is most likely to be on a monthly basis. Another method is for the clerk to operate a petty cash account, whereby the council allocates a fixed amount for a specified period (often a month) from which the clerk reimburses himself. At the end of the specified period, the clerk accounts for the expenditure and the account is made up to the agreed fixed amount. In either case, the clerk should be required to keep a record of the payments with supporting receipts or vouchers.

A clerk who works from home (as most do) also incurs expenses in using his home for council business. The commonest examples are heating, lighting and telephone/

[71]  s. 5, Local Government (Financial Provisions) Act 1963.

fax rental charges. The clerk is commonly reimbursed for these types of expense by a lump sum or periodical payment which is an estimate of their cost to the clerk.

A distinction is drawn between the two types of expense because they are treated differently for the purposes of income tax. The first type of expense, being simply a reimbursement of actual expense incurred on the council's behalf, is not taxable because it cannot include any element of remuneration. Accordingly, it doe not have to be declared to the Inland Revenue in the clerk's tax return.

The second type of expense, being based on an estimate, may contain an element of remuneration and should be declared to the Inland Revenue. So long as the expense was incurred wholly, exclusively and necessarily in the performance of the clerk's duties, it is not taxable.

## Allowances

Many councils provide travel allowances for their clerks when travelling on council business. Where the mode of travel is other than by private car, the allowance should be the actual cost of the travel. The council may attach conditions; for example, it may decide to pay only for standard class rail fares and to meet taxi costs only where there is no practicable alternative form of transport. The allowance for travel by private car is usually based on a rate per mile travelled. The NJC's general conditions of service include mileage rates, which are revised annually. These rates are based on engine capacity; the larger the engine, the higher the rate. There may be an element of profit or remuneration in the NJC rates which is liable to income tax. However, the Inland Revenue also publishes mileage rates, which are slightly lower than the NJC rates, but which do not give rise to a potential tax liability.

The Secretary of State prescribes maximum travel allowances for councillors performing approved duties on behalf of their councils. A council may adopt these for the clerk and other employees.

Many councils also provide subsistence and accommodation allowances where the clerk has to incur the cost of meals, hotels and the like. Again, the Secretary of State prescribes maximum amounts and rates for councillors, which can be applied to clerks.

## FAIR AND UNFAIR DISMISSAL

### The right not to be unfairly dismissed

Subject to certain exclusions (see below), the clerk, as an employee of the council, has a statutory right not to be unfairly dismissed.[72] The right comes into play if the clerk's employment is terminated by the council (whether by notice or not), if his fixed term contract comes to an end and is not renewed under the same contract, or if he terminates the contract (with or without notice) by reason of the council's conduct (i.e. constructive dismissal). In other circumstances, typically where the clerk leaves by mutual agreement with the council, there is no dismissal and the statutory right does not apply.

### Exclusions

The right not to be unfairly dismissed does not apply to:

— employees with less than one year's service (unless the dismissal is automatically unfair – see page 75), ending with the date of termination of the employment; and

— employees who, on or before that date, have reached normal retiring age. If the contract of employment

---

[72]  s. 94, ERA 1996.

specifies a retiring age, that is the normal retiring age. If the contract does not specify a retiring age, then the normal retiring age is 65.

## Fairness

In determining whether or not a dismissal is fair, it is for the council (as employer) to show the reason (or, if more than one, the principal reason) for the clerk's dismissal and that this was of a kind to justify the dismissal of the clerk.[73] A justified reason for dismissal would relate to one or more of the following:

— the clerk was unable or unqualified to do the job (e.g. incapacity through ill health);

— unacceptable conduct (e.g. gross misconduct, unreliability or a poor attendance record);

— redundancy (see below);

— some other substantial reason (e.g. personality clashes, imprisonment).

For a dismissal to be fair, the employer must not only show that the reason for dismissal was fair, but also that he acted reasonably in dismissing the employee rather than, for example, taking some other form of disciplinary action.

In some cases, dismissal is automatically unfair. Those of possible relevance to the clerkship of a local council are:

— being a trade union member;

— not being a trade union member;

— taking part in trade union activities;

---

[73]  s. 98, ERA 1996.

— being pregnant or taking maternity leave;

— taking parental leave;

— taking time off for dependants;

— refusing to work more than the statutory maximum number of hours as prescribed by the Working Time Regulations;

— seeking enforcement of the national minimum wage.

## Redundancy

Dismissal for redundancy occurs where the dismissal is wholly or mainly due to:

— the employer ceasing or intending to cease business, or to cease carrying on the business in the place where the employee works; or

— the employer's need for the employee to carry out the work for which he is employed, or for that work to be carried out where the employee works, ceasing or diminishing.[74]

It is unusual for a clerk to be dismissed for reasons of redundancy because the business of a local council normally cannot cease and very rarely diminishes. However, there have been cases where local councils have surrendered functions to district or unitary authorities with a consequent reduction in business. Where a parish review is carried out by the district or unitary council in England,[75] or a county or county borough council in Wales,[76] there might be alterations to boundaries, or the abolition or

---

[74]  s. 105, ERA 1996.
[75]  Part II, LGRA 1997.
[76]  Part IV, LGA 1972.

amalgamation of parishes or communities. Such changes could lead to staff redundancies in the affected areas. The same could happen following the dissolution of a community council in Wales.[77] In such circumstances, a clerk who loses his post may also be entitled to compensation under the Local Government (Compensation) Regulations 1974.

## Remedies for unfair dismissal

The statutory means of seeking a remedy for unfair dismissal are by way of complaint to an Employment Tribunal. As a general rule, an employee must have been employed for at least a year before qualifying to complain to a tribunal. However, there is no such qualification where the complaint relates to a dismissal which is automatically unfair (except in relation to the transfer of an undertaking to another employer, a situation which is not likely to happen to a clerk).

The tribunal may order reinstatement or re-employment, or the payment of compensation.

Where an employee is made redundant, a statutory scale of payments applies, based on the employee's length of service, as follows:

(a) One and half weeks' pay for each year of employment over the age of 41.

(b) One week's pay for each year of employment over the age of 22.

(c) Half a week's pay for each year of employment where (a) and (b) do not apply.

---

[77]  ss. 28-30, LGA 1972.

Where the employment ends after the employee's 64th birthday, the amount of the payment is reduced.

A council has no power to pay more than the statutory scale of compensation for redundancy.[78]

## PENSIONS AND GRATUITIES

### Pensions

As indicated above (pages 63-64), the council may, but is not obliged to, make provision for the clerk to have a pension. The statutory pension scheme for local government staff is the Local Government Pension Scheme (LGPS).[79] If the council decides to join the LGPS, it must pass a statutory resolution to that effect, of which 28 days' public notice must be given.[80] Once the resolution is passed, the council and the clerk are bound by the terms of the LGPS. It is sensible, therefore, for the council to consult the administering authority (normally the county or unitary council for the area in which the parish or community is situated) before committing itself.

The LGPS is complex, but the essential elements are as follows:

❑ The standard rate of contribution by an employee is 6% of salary and is subject to the Inland Revenue's limit on the amount of contribution which qualifies for tax relief.

❑ In order to receive benefits on retirement, an employee must be in the scheme for at least two years.

---

[78] *Allsop v North Tyneside MBC* (1992) 90 LGR 462.
[79] Local Government Pension Scheme Regulations 1997 (S.I. 1997 No. 1612), as amended.
[80] Reg. B1(1), Local Government Pension Scheme Regulations 1995 (S.I. 1995 No. 1019).

## Pensions and gratuities

❑ The amount of pension is

$$\frac{\text{the employee's total period of membership}}{80} \text{ x final salary}$$

❑ The amount of an employee's retirement grant is

$$\frac{3 \text{ x total period of membership}}{80} \text{ x final salary}$$

❑ If an employee retires at or after the normal retirement age of 65, he is entitled to both a pension and a retirement grant.

❑ There are provisions for paying a death grant to dependants when an employee dies in service and for paying a pension to a former employee's surviving spouse.

❑ An employee can (at the discretion of his employer) increase the amount of his pension by adding years (if retiring over the age of 50) and by increasing contributions (if retiring over the age of 55).

❑ There are provisions enabling an employee to make additional voluntary contributions (AVCs) and for the transferring of the value of pension contributions made to other pension funds into the scheme.

❑ The employer's contribution is calculated by actuarial valuation as at 31st March 1998 and thereafter at three yearly intervals. This means that the employer's contribution will vary, depending on the performance of the pension fund.

❑ If an employee makes extra payments for added years, the employer's additional contributions to the fund are measured in accordance with guidance given by the Government Actuary.

❑ The employer is required to pay its contributions and those of its employees into the fund maintained by the administering authority.

## Gratuities

If the council does not make pension arrangements, it may, on termination of the clerk's employment, pay the clerk a gratuity.[81] This is a purely discretionary payment and the council cannot lawfully bind itself to make such a payment. A decision to make a gratuity payment does not require a special resolution (as in the case of a decision to join the LGPS – see above).

There are three types of gratuity: death-in-service, retirement and redundancy. The main provisions relating to each type of gratuity are as follows:

### Death-in-service

Where the clerk has been employed for at least one year and dies in service, the council may pay a gratuity to one or more of the clerk's spouse and dependants. The gratuity may be a lump sum or an annuity, or both. If paid to more than one person, the total paid must not exceed the statutorily prescribed maximum.

The maximum amount of a death benefit gratuity (including the capital value of an annuity) is 3.75% of the aggregate of the following:

❑ The clerk's annual rate of remuneration at the date of death times the total length of service in years and days before 1st April 1987 and 50% of any war service during which the clerk might have been in post.

---

[81] Local Government (Discretionary Payments) Regulations 1996 (S.I. 1996 No. 1680), as amended.

❑ The clerk's annual rate of remuneration at the date of death times the length of service in years and days after 31st March 1987, but in the case of a clerk (i) whose contractual weekly hours of work were fewer than 15 and who was under 50 on 16th August 1993 or (ii) whose contractual weekly hours were at least 15 and who was 55 or over on 1st April 1987, disregarding any assumed membership.

"Assumed membership" relates to membership of the LGPS. For the purposes of the 1996 Regulations, the person in respect of whose employment a gratuity is paid is assumed to have been a member of the LGPS, unless he would have been disqualified from membership. This complicated and obscure provision appears to mean that the period of service of a clerk which falls into categories (i) and (ii) above is not counted in calculating the number of years' service on which the maximum amount of the gratuity is based.

The "annual rate of remuneration" is the highest rate of pay on:

— the date of ceasing to be employed; or

— 12 months before that date; or

— 24 months before that date.

In calculating the maximum amount in accordance with the foregoing, any earnings between the lower and upper earnings limits for national insurance purposes are disregarded. The national insurance limits are set by the Government each fiscal year (for the year 2000-2001 the lower earnings limit is £76 per week and the upper earnings limit is £535 per week). Most clerks are likely to be paid a salary which is below the upper earnings limit. This means that the maximum gratuity payable by a council will, in the majority of cases, be calculated by reference to the lower earnings limit.

The maximum period of service which may be taken into account is 40 years, and service under the age of 16 and over the age of 70 is disregarded.

An example of the calculation required to determine the maximum amount of gratuity which may be paid is –

A clerk, who is paid £5,000 p.a., dies on 1st August 2000 at the age of 65 after 10 years' service. The maximum gratuity payable to his dependants is:

£3,952 (the lower earnings limit) x 10 x 3.75% = £1,482

*Retirement*

A gratuity may be paid to a clerk on retirement provided that he has been employed:

(a) for at least five years; or

(b) for at least one year and is aged 60 or over, or is unable to carry out the duties of the post efficiently because of permanent ill-health or infirmity of mind or body.

The clerk cannot receive a retirement gratuity if a redundancy gratuity has been paid (see below).

A retirement gratuity may consist of a lump sum or an annuity, or both.

The maximum amount of a retirement gratuity (including the capital value of an annuity) is either: (i) three eightieths of the clerk's annual remuneration for each year of service, or (ii) the prescribed maximum.

The prescribed maximum is the same as for a death-in-service gratuity (see above).

Where a retirement annuity is paid and the original annuitant dies and the capital value of the annuity paid before death is less than the capital value of the annuity when granted, a further annuity may be paid to the annuitant's spouse and dependants. The maximum amount payable in respect of the second annuity is the lesser of:

(a) the shortfall in capital value; or

(b) two-thirds of the amount of the annuity paid to the original annuitant.

An example of the calculations required to determine the maximum gratuity payable on retirement is as follows–

> A clerk retires on 1st August 2000 after 20 years' service. His final salary at retirement is £15,000 p.a.
>
> 1. Calculation based on 3/80ths of final salary:
>
>    £15,000 x 20 x 3/80 = £11,250
>
> 2. Calculation based on the prescribed maximum:
>
>    £3,952 (the lower earnings limit) x 20 x 3.75% = £2,964
>
> The maximum gratuity payable is therefore £11,250.

## Redundancy

The council may pay a gratuity to the clerk when his employment is ended by reason of redundancy or in the interests of the efficient exercise of the council's functions. The clerk must have been employed for at least five years or, if aged 60 or over, at least one year. The gratuity may be paid as a lump sum or as an annuity, or both.

The maximum amount of the gratuity (including the capital value of an annuity) must not exceed the prescribed maximum, which is the same as for a death-in-service and a retirement gratuity.

There are provisions very similar to those relating to a retirement gratuity covering the payment of a further gratuity or annuity to a spouse and dependants on the death of the annuitant.

### Approval by the Inland Revenue

Before paying a gratuity, a council should obtain approval from the Pensions Schemes Office of the Inland Revenue (for address, see Appendix 5 below, page 131) so that the payment can be made free of income tax and national insurance deductions. The Inland Revenue normally issues the following advice to councils in response to requests for approval:

> "The Pensions Scheme Office will grant tax approval to a scheme providing gratuities on retirement (including retirement due to ill health) and/or death in service. The provisions are incorporated in Part VI of the Local Government (Discretionary Payment) Regulations 1996.
>
> The governing Regulations also include provision to pay gratuities on redundancy; however, due to the nature of the tax legislation our approval cannot extend tax relief to these gratuities. If your council wishes to pay redundancy gratuities you can of course set up a separate scheme and any payments will be considered separately by the Inspector of Taxes for tax relief.
>
> In order that [we] can grant formal approval to retirement and death in service gratuities, [we] need to see a signed council resolution showing that these gratuities will be calculated and paid in accordance with the terms of the 1996 Regulations. As explained above, this resolution should exclude redundancy gratuities.

The maximum approvable gratuity is calculated by the formula 3.75% x actual final earnings x service, but service only counts up to the age of 70 and must not exceed 40 years. The gratuity can be paid as a lump sum, converted to an annuity or paid as a combination of both. Once tax approval has been granted a lump sum gratuity will be tax and NIC free. However, if the gratuity is paid in annuity form, the annuity payments will, like a pension, be subject to tax."

More detailed information on pensions and gratuities is available from the Local Government Pension Committee at the NJC (for address, see Appendix 5).

## HEALTH AND SAFETY

As an employer, the council has a general statutory duty to ensure, so far as is reasonably practicable, the health, safety and welfare at work of all its employees.[82] There is a similar duty on employees at work (a) to take reasonable care for the health and safety of themselves and of others who may be affected by their acts or omissions at work, and (b) to co-operate with their employer so far as is necessary to enable the employer to comply with his statutory duty.[83]

Detailed regulations have been made by the Secretary of State covering many aspects of health and safety at work and the regulatory body, the Health and Safety Executive (for address, see Appendix 5 below, page 131), has issued codes of practice and a great deal of guidance to employers and employees. The main areas with which local council clerks are likely to be concerned are:

---

[82]  s. 2, Health and Safety at Work etc. Act 1974.
[83]  s. 7, Health and Safety at Work etc. Act 1974.

— Management of Health and Safety at Work: approved code of practice;

— Display Screen Equipment at Work: guidance on regulations;

— Workplace Health, Safety and Welfare: approved code of practice.

Where a council has more than five employees, it must prepare and, as often as appropriate, revise a written health and safety policy for its employees. It will usually fall to the clerk to draft the policy for the council to approve. Once approved, the council must ensure that the policy is brought to the attention of the employees.[84] An example of a health and safety policy adopted by a town council can be viewed via the SLCC website (for address, see Appendix 5 below, page 132).

Under the common law, too, an employer has an overall duty to take reasonable care for its employees at work. This is reinforced by the obligation on local councils to insure against liability for bodily injury or disease sustained by their employees.[85] The level of insurance cover must be at least £5 million.[86]

---

[84] s. 2(3), Health and Safety at Work etc. Act 1974.
[85] Employers' Liability (Compulsory Insurance) Act 1969.
[86] Reg. 3(1), Employers' Liability (Compulsory Insurance) Regulations 1998 (S.I. 1998 No. 2573).

CHAPTER 4

# QUALIFICATIONS, TRAINING AND SKILLS

## *QUALIFICATIONS*

A clerk is not required by law to have any particular academic qualifications. Most clerks probably have none that are specifically relevant to local council work, although many have qualifications of one sort or another. However, in the last ten years or so, courses have been developed which lead to an academic qualification of particular suitability for a local council clerk.

## *LOCAL POLICY COURSES*

Local policy courses are run by the Department of Local Policy at the Cheltenham and Gloucester College of Higher Education (see Appendix 5 for address). The courses are modular, so that a student may study any number of modules from one up to the maximum (currently ten).

The modules are:

- Procedures for Local Council Administration (EL 110)
- Community and Locality (EL 105)
- Law for Local Councils (EL 111)
- Environment and Society (EL 100)
- The Decision Makers (EL 103)
- Project Management (EL 108)
- Finance and Resources for Community Organisations (EL 109)
- Management at Work (EL 102)
- Town and Country Planning (EL 104)
- Action with Communities (EL 106).

## Level One: The Certificate of Higher Education

This is a first level course which focuses on the local neighbourhood and the work of local councils. It is particularly suitable for clerks of local councils.

The Certificate (CertHE) is awarded on the successful completion of the 10 modules listed above. The course requires about 1,000 hours of study. A full-time student would take a year to complete the course and a part-time student between two and three years.

If the clerk is paid in accordance with the LC scale agreed between SLCC and NALC (see Chapter 3 "Employment Contract and Job Description", page 58 above), the award of a CertHE entitles the clerk to two pay increments.

## College Certificate

A clerk who chooses not to study all ten modules, but completes five successfully, will be awarded a College Certificate. If the clerk is paid in accordance with the LC scale agreed between SLCC and NALC (see Chapter 3 "Employment Contract", page 58 above), one pay increment is earned when the Certificate is awarded.

A part-time student will normally take one to two years to complete the five modules.

## Levels Two and Three: BA Honours Degree

Once the CertHE course has been successfully completed, a student may go on to Level Two. The focus of this course is on advanced levels of practice and comparative studies of activities in different parts of the country.

At Level Three, more emphasis is placed on academic skills, including the investigation and analysis of a specialist subject and the presentation of information and ideas in a dissertation.

Successful completion of Levels Two and Three leads to the award of a BA Honours Degree. A clerk who is awarded a Degree is also entitled to two further pay increments on the LC scale agreed between SLCC and NALC (see above).

## Course delivery

The local policy course has four elements –

❑ **Course material:** at Level One this includes home study course books containing information, written discussion and activities.

❑ **Assessment programme:** this is designed to check on what has been learned and to give an additional opportunity for learning through a variety of assignments. There are one or two assignments for each module, involving written reports, problem solving projects and local investigations.

❑ **Residential schools:** there are two residential schools in the year, usually in October and February, held from noon on Friday until noon on Sunday.

❑ **Tutorial support:** this is provided by a team of tutors in locations around the country.

The academic year is divided into two semesters, starting in October and February. Two modules are taught in each semester.

## Finance

The fees for the full CertHE course for a local council clerk are based on the size of population served by the local council. They are currently (October 2000) as follows –

- Population less than 4,000 – £1,000
- Population 4,000 to 8,000 – £1,300
- Population over 8,000 – £1,600.

Fees can be paid over two years in instalments.

The fees cover registration, course books, assessment and award fees, teaching from local and national tutors including residential school programmes, access to college administration and course development. The cost of accommodation at residential schools is extra.

It is normal for a local council to give financial support for the training of its clerk, by paying all or some of the fees and the cost of course materials or activities.

A few councils now require applicants for the post of clerk to have one or more of the local policy qualifications, or an equivalent qualification. These are mostly town councils or larger parish/community councils.

Whilst it may be relatively uncommon for a council to require its clerk to have a local policy qualification, it is becoming less rare for councils to require a clerk to seek to acquire one. It is also becoming more common for a council to encourage and give financial support to a clerk who wishes to take a local policy course.

### TRAINING

Not all clerks need or aspire to academic qualifications. However, all clerks (including those with such qualifications) will benefit from regular training in the skills required to perform their role properly. Training can take many forms: for example, attendance at day courses, weekend schools, conferences, informal meetings of clerks and others and the study of specific topics (e.g. book-keeping and accountancy, computer skills, business management).

Whilst there is no national course available for clerks which leads to a formal qualification, other than the local policy courses, various organisations provide training courses on particular subjects or themes.

The regional councils of the National Joint Council for Local Government Services (for the address, see Appendix 5) sometimes run courses for local council clerks, the successful completion of which is recognised by the grant of a certificate.

The Society of Local Council Clerks, the National Association of Local Councils and county associations of local councils all run courses, conferences and training seminars. (For the addresses of SLCC and NALC, see Appendix 5. The addresses of the county associations of local councils can be obtained from NALC and can be viewed on the NALC website.) Some district, unitary and county councils also run courses and conferences for local council members and clerks.

Obtaining qualifications and undertaking training require a considerable commitment on the part of the clerk, beyond the performance of his ordinary duties. Courses, conferences, etc. also have to be paid for. It should be normal practice for the council either to pay the whole cost, or to make a substantial contribution towards the cost. The council will benefit from the additional skills and knowledge which the clerk will be able to bring to the job. The clerk will, at the very least, obtain greater job satisfaction and thus work more effectively. Some councils have argued against contributing to the cost of the training of clerks on the ground that, once better qualified or trained, a clerk will move to another job. This is, to say the least, a short-sighted view. The more clerks who are properly qualified and trained, the better served will be local councils generally.

## SKILLS

### Management and office skills

Apart from formal qualifications and training, a competent and effective clerk needs a wide range of skills. Basic literacy and numeracy skills are obviously necessary, since much of the day-to-day work of a clerk involves writing letters, minutes, reports, etc. and keeping financial records. Other key skills are those relevant to office procedures and administration. Perhaps the most important skills lie in the field of computing and word processing. It is probably not going too far to say that all local council clerks ought to be familiar with the use of computers, at least for the production of letters and other documents.

Familiarity with other administrative aids, such as telephone answering machines and services, copiers, fax and email, is also desirable. An increasing number of councils have a website, which the clerk is probably expected to manage and keep up to date.

### Personal qualities and relationships with councillors and others

The clerk is usually the only employee of the council and is, in effect, its chief executive. He or she is responsible for carrying out the policies and decisions of the council. It is therefore important the clerk and the councillors work closely and harmoniously together. It is even more important that there should be close co-operation between the clerk and the chairman. Without both parties fully understanding their respective roles, disagreements and misunderstandings may arise. It has been suggested that there is a large annual turnover of clerks; regrettably, a significant proportion of the turnover results from the resignation or dismissal of clerks because of a failure to establish a proper working relationship with their councils or chairmen.

As the council's chief executive, the clerk will come into contact with persons from all walks of life. As indicated in Chapter 2, The Role of the Clerk (above pages 47-48), a good working relationship between the clerk and officers of other local authorities, agencies and organisations with which the council regularly deals is very important. In addition, an ability to deal with members of the public, particularly in handling complaints, is highly desirable.

A clerk therefore needs to have the personal qualities which are conducive to co-operation and mutual understanding. These include (in no particular order) tact, patience, politeness, tolerance and integrity.

# CHAPTER 5

# THE LEGAL STATUS OF LOCAL COUNCILS

## THE CONSTITUTIONAL AND LEGAL POSITION OF LOCAL COUNCILS

### The constitutional position

The system of rural parishes and parish councils in England and Wales was established by the Local Government Act 1894. Under this Act, most of the civil functions of the Church of England and other bodies were transferred to the new councils, which were created only in rural areas. Parishes were grouped in rural districts (also created by the 1894 Act). Since then, the basic parish structure has remained the same, although there have been many detailed changes, the most important of which are as follows –

❏ **The Local Government Act 1972** (in force from 1st April 1974) continued parishes in England, but in Wales replaced them with communities, which inherited most of the powers and functions of the former parishes. A large number of municipal boroughs and urban districts were abolished, with many of them being re-created as parishes or communities with parish or community councils. Parish and community councils were empowered to call themselves towns and to designate their chairmen as town mayors. Whilst the whole of Wales was divided into communities, the parish system was not automatically extended to urban areas in England. However, the Act established the procedure by which new parishes could be created everywhere in England, except in Greater London. A number of new functions were conferred on parish and community councils and most of the limitations on their expenditure were abolished. Rural districts were abolished and largely replaced by districts which combined both urban and rural areas.

❏ **The Local Government Finance Acts of 1982 and 1992** reformed the financial rules applicable to parish and community council budgets, accounts and audit. (The 1982 Act has been replaced by the Audit Commission Act 1998, a consolidating statute which does not change the law.)

❏ **The Local Government Act 1992** created the Local Government Commission for England with a remit to review the local government areas in England created by the LGA 1972. The Commission's reviews led to the abolition of some county and district councils and their replacement by so-called unitary authorities, combining the functions of both counties and districts. The Commission also recommended the creation of some 50 new parishes, mostly in urban areas, many of which have since been created by Ministerial order.

❏ **The Local Government (Wales) Act 1994** (in force from 1st April 1996) reorganised the principal tier of local government in Wales by abolishing the county and district councils and replacing them with single-tier county and county borough councils, combining the functions of the abolished authorities. The Act did not change the structure or powers of community councils but altered the rules concerning their creation and dissolution. The Act also gave the Secretary of State for Wales power to direct principal authorities to consult community councils on designated matters (a power which is unlikely to be exercised if voluntary consultation arrangements are put in place).

❏ **The Local Government and Rating Act 1997** made new provision for the alteration of parishes and for the creation of new parishes following a petition by local electors. The Act gave the Secretary of State for the Environment, Transport and the Regions effectively identical powers to those of the Secretary of State for Wales to direct principal authorities in England to consult parish councils. The Act also conferred new powers on parish and community councils in the fields of transport, traffic calming and crime prevention.

❏ **The Government of Wales Act 1998** made provision for the transfer of the regulatory and other powers of the Secretary of State for Wales relating to community councils to the National Assembly for Wales. The transfer took place on 1st July 1999.

❏ **The Local Government Act 2000** introduced a new ethical system for local government councillors and employees.

### The legal position

Parish and community councils are statutory corporations.[87] Whilst they have no physical existence, they have a separate legal personality apart from their members. They never die and therefore exist in perpetuity (unless abolished by or under statute). This means that:

– the acts of a council are distinct from the acts of its members;

– normally, the members are not personally liable should the acts of the council have some adverse legal effect.[88]

Thus, if the council breaks a contract, the other party must seek a remedy from the council, not from the councillors.

---

[87] ss. 14(2) and 33(1), LGA 1972.
[88] s. 265, Public Health Act 1875, as amended.

The powers of statutory corporations are limited. Local councils only have the following powers:

— those expressly conferred by or under statute; or

— those which arise by necessary implication; or

— those which are reasonably incidental or conducive to the exercise of express statutory powers.

The express powers of local councils are to be found in statutes and statutory instruments. The powers which arise by necessary implication, or which are reasonably conducive to the exercise of express statutory powers, were originally derived from the common law (i.e. the law developed by the courts). However, to a large extent these subsidiary powers are now contained in section 111 of the Local Government Act 1972 and it is not often necessary to rely on the common law to provide lawful authority for the acts of local councils.

Apart from these limitations, the courts have developed a rule that, even if a local council apparently acts within its legal powers, the council will be acting unlawfully if its actions are clearly unreasonable. The principles upon which councils have to act to be "reasonable" are known as the "Wednesbury principles", having been laid down in the case of *Associated Provincial Picture Houses v Wednesbury Corporation* [1948] KB 223. The principles require that, where a council is given a discretionary power, the council must in exercising that power only have regard to relevant matters, must disregard irrelevant matters and must come to a decision which a council could reasonably have reached. Thus the courts have, for example, struck down decisions by local authorities to pay excessive wages, to refuse to stock a daily newspaper in their libraries for political reasons and to ban stag hunting on council land for moral reasons.

If a council acts outside its powers, it is said to act *ultra vires* (Latin for "beyond the powers"). The legal consequences are, or may be:

— any contract made by the council when so acting is void and therefore unenforceable (e.g. to guarantee a loan taken out by a company set up by the council to provide leisure facilities, partly if not wholly to evade statutory controls on borrowing);

— legal action may be taken against the council by an elector, or other person with a sufficient interest in the matter, to quash any decision already taken or to restrain any future *ultra vires* action;

— if unlawful expenditure has been incurred, the auditor may apply to the court for a declaration to that effect and may seek to recover any such payment from those responsible (usually some or all of the councillors);[89]

— if unlawful expenditure is likely to be incurred, the auditor may issue a prohibition order to prevent such expenditure.[90]

## The powers of local councils

The specific statutory powers of local councils are scattered throughout a large number of statutes and statutory instruments. A summary of the main powers is set out in Appendix 4. More details will also be found in the books suggested for further reading (see Appendix 7).

---

[89] s. 17(1), ACA 1998.
[90] s. 20, ACA 1998.

Almost without exception, the powers vested in local councils are discretionary.[91] There is no statutory duty on a council to exercise all or any of them. A decision whether or not to exercise a power is thus one of policy for the council to take; it is not a matter of law, where an external authority can require the council to make a decision. However, any decision of a council to exercise or not to exercise a power is subject to the "Wednesbury principles" and to the doctrine of *ultra vires* described above. These limitations may operate to restrain action which would otherwise be lawful, and also to require action which is necessary in the interests of the local inhabitants.

Despite generally having discretion as to whether or not it exercises a power, a council may be bound by contract or by a similar legal obligation to act, or not to act, in a particular way; to that extent its discretion may be fettered.

## The procedures of local councils

Although the powers of local councils are largely discretionary, the statutory procedures under which they operate are largely mandatory. The reason is that local councils are public bodies, answerable to the local community and mainly financed by a compulsory levy on council tax payers.

In some cases, the relevant statute or statutory instrument provides a sanction for a breach of procedure (e.g. it is a summary offence for a person having custody of council minutes to obstruct a person who is entitled to inspect

---

[91] The two exceptions are: 1. If in the opinion of the council there is a demand for allotments, the council is obliged to meet that demand (s. 23(1), Smallholding and Allotments Act 1908); 2. Where responsibility for a closed churchyard is transferred to a parish council, the council is under an obligation to maintain the churchyard in decent order (s. 215, LGA 1972).

them).[92] In others, there is no specific sanction (e.g. the rules relating to the calling and holding of meetings).[93] In such cases, those that wish to mount a legal challenge to the validity of a decision, or omission, by a council will have to take appropriate legal action, usually by way of judicial review in the High Court.

Where a council is alleged to be in breach of the "Wednesbury principles" or the doctrine of *ultra vires*, again a legal challenge can be made through the courts.

Local councils are not subject to the jurisdiction of the Commissioner for Local Administration (the Local Ombudsman) so that there is no regulatory body to which a person can complain about the activities of a local council. For this reason, and in the general interests of openness and fairness, every council should have a procedure for dealing with complaints. NALC recommends a procedure to its member councils and a council cannot go far wrong if it adopts that procedure. However, the new Standards Boards being set up under the Local Government Act 2000 will be able to investigate complaints against councillors – see Appendix 8.

## THE ROLE OF LOCAL COUNCILS

In the White Paper *Modern Local Government – In Touch with the People*, published in July 1998, the Secretary of State for the Environment, Transport and the Regions gave strong backing to the role of local councils in England, as the following extracts show –

> "[Parish councils] are an essential part of the structure of local democracy in our country. Parish councils will

---

[92]  s. 228(7), LGA 1972.
[93]  Sch.12, LGA 1972.

continue to play a key role in many of our towns and villages. They have a vital role in helping principal councils keep in touch with the smallest communities in their areas. Parish councils can work in partnership with their principal council to bring government closer to the people, and to establish the decentralised delivery of local government services. It is important therefore that parish councils everywhere embrace the new culture of openness and accountability, putting their local people first." (Paragraph 2.14)

"The Government wishes to see consultation and participation embedded into the culture of all councils, including parishes, and undertaken across a wide range of each council's responsibilities." (Paragraph 4.6)

Very similar sentiments were expressed by the Secretary of State for Wales in the contemporaneous White Paper *Local Voices – Modernising Local Government in Wales* (paragraph 2.22).

## Representation, consultation and service delivery

The foregoing extracts from the 1998 White Paper highlight areas where local councils can play a role:

— representation (keeping principal councils, and other agencies and bodies, in touch with local communities);

— consultation, both by principal councils and others and of the local community; and

— local delivery of services (normally in partnership with principal councils).

However, local councils are not restricted to co-operation with principal authorities. They also have a role to play in co-operating with and assisting other bodies (such as local voluntary organisations and charities) and in representing the views of their local communities wherever the council thinks it is necessary to do so.

Local councils have statutory rights to be consulted or to be notified in relation to some specific matters, notably in the fields of planning and rights of way. These are summarised in Appendix 4. In other cases, local councils will have to seek agreement with those by whom they wish to be consulted or notified. So far as principal authorities are concerned, there are statutory provisions giving the Secretary of State and the National Assembly for Wales power to direct consultation with local councils. Those powers are regarded as ones of last resort and will only be used if voluntary consultation arrangements are not put in place. The existence of those powers has prompted many principal councils to make consultative arrangements with the parishes or communities in their areas. An example from Wiltshire is in Appendix 6.

Local councils also have an important representative role. As the local elected bodies they can, and normally should, seek to represent to other persons and bodies the views of the parish, community or town. Local councils will often have representatives on the committees of local charities and voluntary organisations. Some of their members may also be members of principal authorities and thus able to represent directly to those other authorities.

## EMPLOYMENT OF OFFICERS BY LOCAL COUNCILS

A local council has power to appoint such officers as it thinks necessary for the proper discharge of its functions.[94] An officer appointed by the council holds office on such

---

[94]   s. 112(1), LGA 1972.

reasonable terms and conditions, including conditions relating to remuneration, as the council thinks fit.[95]

Any paid officer or employee appointed by the council must be appointed on merit, but subject to the provisions of:

— sections 5 and 6 of the Disability Discrimination Act 1995 (meaning of discrimination and duty to make adjustments);

— section 7 of the Sex Discrimination Act 1975 (discrimination permitted in relation to employment where the sex of the employee is a genuine occupational qualification);

— section 7 of the Race Relations Act 1976 (discrimination permitted in relation to employment where being of a particular racial group is a genuine occupational qualification).[96]

The effect of the foregoing provisions is that, like most employers, a local council must not discriminate against its employees and officers on grounds of disability, sex or race. It cannot be argued that being of a particular sex or race is a genuine occupational qualification for the post of local council clerk. (In this context, it is worth drawing attention to the fact that the English and the Welsh are distinct racial groups. The relevance of this is that a council which required its clerk to be English or Welsh would be in breach of the 1976 Act. However, a requirement that the clerk of a community council in Wales must be a Welsh speaker would not be in breach of the 1976 Act because a person does not have to be Welsh to be a speaker of the language.)

---

[95]  s. 112(2), LGA 1972.
[96]  s. 7(1) and (2), LGHA 1989, as amended.

A council has power to delegate the discharge of any of its functions (with some exceptions) to an officer, although this does not prevent the council from exercising those functions.[97] The exception relevant to a local council is that the council's functions in relation to the issuing of a precept or to the borrowing of money must be carried out by the council itself.[98] In practice, most of the administrative functions of a council (e.g. dealing with correspondence, collection of rents and hire charges) are delegated to the clerk.

### EMPLOYMENT OF COUNCILLOR AS CLERK

A local council also has power to appoint one of its members (i.e. a councillor) as unpaid clerk.[99] Such an appointment does not, as a matter of statutory obligation, have to be on merit. As a general rule, it is undesirable for a councillor also to be the clerk of the council of which he is a member, except on a temporary or acting basis whilst the council is without a paid clerk. A councillor cannot participate fully and effectively in council and committee meetings when he is also responsible for taking the notes which will form the minutes. There may also be a conflict of interest between the roles of councillor and clerk, in that a councillor/clerk may wish the council to pursue a matter but the council may decline to do so. As clerk, the councillor's loyalty and responsibility must be to the council, and his personal interest will have to be pursued (if at all) by other means.

A councillor cannot be appointed as paid clerk (or other paid officer) of the council of which he is a member while still a councillor and for twelve months after ceasing to be

---

[97]  s. 101, LGA 1972.
[98]  s. 101(6), LGA 1972.
[99]  s. 112(5), LGA 1972.

one.[100] This means that, if a councillor wishes to seek appointment as paid clerk, he must first resign and then wait a year before taking up the paid post. In the interim, the council may appoint the councillor as unpaid clerk. However, the council must ensure that the councillor is not appointed to a paid clerkship for that period, even without receiving any pay. That would be unlawful, because an office can still be a "paid office" even if payment is waived.

The council cannot guarantee that an ex-councillor will be appointed as paid clerk, even if he has previously served as unpaid clerk. When the clerkship falls vacant, the council must appoint a post-holder on merit,[101] which means in practice that the post has to be advertised and an ex-councillor treated no differently from other applicants.

It is not unknown for a councillor to be the clerk of a council of which he is not a member. There is no legal barrier to a councillor being so appointed, so long as the appointment is on merit.

---

[100] s. 116, LGA 1972.
[101] s. 7(1), LGHA 1989.

# APPENDICES

# SPECIMEN CONTRACT AND STATEMENT OF PARTICULARS OF EMPLOYMENT

## 1. Employer and employee

1.1 The Employer is [name of council] of [address] and is referred to as the Council.

1.2 The Employee is [name and address] and is referred to as the Clerk.

## 2. Commencement

2.1 The Clerk's employment commenced on [date].

## 3. Continuous service

3.1 Employment with any other employer shall not count as part of the Clerk's continuous period of employment with the council [except where the previous employer was a local authority].

## 4. Job title

4.1 The title of the job for which the Clerk is employed is Clerk to the [name of council].

4.2 The duties of the Clerk are described in the job description attached to this contract.

4.3 The job description may be altered by the council and, in addition to the duties set out in it, the Clerk may from time to time be required to perform such further or other duties as the Council may reasonably determine.

4.4 The Clerk is the Proper Office of the Council.

## 5. Salary and expenses

5.1 The Clerk's commencing salary is £[amount] per [week] [month] [quarter] [year] in accordance with the salary scales agreed between the Society of Local Council Clerks and the National Association of Local Councils (referred to as the LC Scale) at LC Scale [number] and Spinal Column point [number].

5.2 The Clerk will be paid by [cheque] [bank transfer] at [weekly] [monthly] [quarterly] intervals starting from the commencement of employment.

5.3 The Clerk will be entitled to reclaim expenses necessarily incurred in performing [his] [her] duties and such other expenses as are payable in accordance with the general conditions of service referred to in paragraph 17 of this contract.

5.4 Expenses will be paid or reimbursed only on presentation of appropriate receipts at the same intervals as the Clerk's salary is paid.

## 6. Hours of work

6.1 The Clerk's normal hours of work are [state number] per [week] [month] [if full time state days of work, e.g. Monday to Friday] and shall include attendance at Council, committee and other meetings related to Council business.

6.2 The Clerk will be required to attend Council and other meetings in the evening and at weekends as necessary.

## 7. Place of work

7.1 The Clerk's usual place of work is [address: usually the clerk's home if part-time or otherwise the Council's offices] but [he] [she] may be required to work at [place] on specified occasions.

## 8. Holidays and holiday pay

8.1 The Clerk is entitled to [number] weeks' paid holiday per year on a *pro rata* basis according to the number of hours worked each week [together with normal Bank or Public Holidays]. The year runs from 1st April until the following 31st March.

8.2 The Clerk will be paid [his] [her] normal salary during holiday periods.

8.3 The Clerk's holidays will be taken at a time or at times agreed with the Council.

8.4 Where the Clerk's employment with the Council begins or ends during the year [he] [she] will be entitled to a proportion of the full paid holiday entitlement depending upon the length of the period of the year which has passed or remains to come.

## 9. Absence through sickness or injury

9.1 When the Clerk is absent from work through sickness or injury, the Council must be informed as soon as possible and the reason for absence given.

9.2 If the Clerk is absent for more than [number] working days [he] [she] must provide a medical certificate giving the reason for absence and must provide further medical certificates for each week of absence.

9.3 The Clerk will be paid [his] [her] normal salary [less

any Statutory Sick Pay or other social security benefits received] for [number] [days] [weeks] during the year, as defined in clause 8.1 above.

## 10. Pension

10.1 [The Council is a member of the Local Government Pension Scheme and the Clerk is entitled to join the Scheme as an active member.] [The Council is not a member of the Local Government Pension Scheme and no pension arrangements for the Clerk are in force.]

## [11. Supervision of staff

11.1 Where the Clerk supervises other Council employees [he] [she] will be paid the appropriate supplement in accordance with the LC scale.]

## 12. Recognition of qualifications

12.1 The Council will pay the Clerk the additional salary on attaining one or more of the qualifications specified in the LC Scale.

## 13. Grievance procedure

13.1 If the Clerk has any grievance arising from or relating to [his] [her] employment, [he] [she] shall in the first instance give written details to the Chairman of the Council. If the grievance cannot be resolved by agreement between the Clerk and the Chairman, the Chairman shall report the matter to the Council. The Council shall give the Clerk the opportunity to address the Council, either personally or through a representative, before deciding what action to take.

13.2 In dealing with a grievance matter, the Council will have regard to the Advisory, Conciliation and

Arbitration Service (ACAS) Code of Practice on Grievance and Disciplinary Procedures.

## 14. Disciplinary procedure

14.1 Where the Council proposes to take disciplinary action against the Clerk, [he] [she] shall be given full details in writing of the misconduct or other disciplinary matter alleged against [him] [her]. The Clerk shall be given an opportunity to respond to the allegations, either in person or through a representative, both in writing and orally before the Council decides what action to take.

14.2 In dealing with a disciplinary matter, the Council will have regard to the ACAS Code of Practice on Grievance and Disciplinary Procedures.

14.3 Where the Council considers that the Clerk is guilty of gross misconduct, it may dismiss the Clerk without notice and without recourse to the foregoing procedures.

Gross misconduct includes the following:

- Theft, fraud, deliberate falsification of records
- Assault on another person
- Deliberate damage to Council property
- Serious incapacity through alcohol or being under the influence of illegal drugs
- Serious negligence which causes unacceptable loss, injury or damage to Council property.

## 15. Termination of employment

15.1 The Clerk shall give the Council at least [number] months' notice in writing to terminate this contract.

15.2 The Council shall give the Clerk written notice to terminate this contract as follows:

- During the first year of continuous employment, one month
- Thereafter the period of notice shall be increased by one week for each year of continuous employment up to a maximum of 12 weeks' notice after 12 years of continuous employment.

## [16. Retirement age

16.1 The normal retirement age for the Clerk is 65.]

## 17. General conditions of service

17.1 Subject to the foregoing provisions hereof, the Conditions of Service of the National Joint Council for Local Government Services apply to this contract.

## 18. Acknowledgement

18.1 The Clerk hereby acknowledges that this contract contains the particulars of employment required by section 1 of the Employment Rights Act 1996 to be provided to every employee within two months of the commencement of employment.

Signed on behalf of the Council:

Signed by the Clerk:

Date:

*[Note: it is desirable that two copies of the contract are prepared, signed and dated so that both the Council and the Clerk have a copy.]*

# SPECIMEN JOB DESCRIPTION FOR THE CLERK OF THE COUNCIL

1. The clerk is the proper officer of the council and will carry out all the functions conferred on the proper officer by statute or otherwise.

2. The clerk will be responsible for ensuring that the statutory and other provisions governing the administration of the council and its affairs are complied with.

3. The clerk will prepare the agendas for meetings of the council, will attend such meetings and will prepare the minutes of such meetings for submission to the council for approval.

4. The clerk will likewise prepare the agendas for, attend and prepare the minutes of committee and sub-committee meetings.

5. [England] The clerk will prepare the agendas for, attend and prepare the minutes of the annual [parish] [town] meeting and any other [parish] [town] meetings held during the year.

   [Wales] The clerk will prepare the agendas for, attend and prepare the minutes of any community meetings held during the year.

6. The clerk is the responsible financial officer of the council and will prepare and maintain the accounts and other financial records of the council (including those relating to Value Added Tax) in accordance with all

statutory and other accounting and audit requirements and practices.

7.  The clerk will be responsible for the deduction of income tax and national insurance contributions from the remuneration of the council's employees (including that of the clerk) and payment of the same to the Inland Revenue.

8.  The clerk will be responsible for ensuring that all decisions of the council, its committees and sub-committees are carried out promptly and accurately.

9.  The clerk will be responsible for receiving all correspondence and other documentation on behalf of the council and for ensuring that the same is brought before the council or its relevant committees or sub-committees as necessary.

10. The clerk will, if so required by the council, review and report on the policies of the council and how effectively they are being implemented, having regard to the principles of "best value" prescribed by or under statute.

11. The clerk will be responsible for supervising other staff employed by the council and ensuring that relevant statutory provisions covering the terms and conditions of employment of staff are observed.

12. Where the council employs five or more staff, the clerk will be responsible for preparing a health and safety policy and submitting it to the council for approval.

13. If so required by the council, the clerk will act as a representative of the council at conferences, meetings, public inquiries and other similar events.

14. The clerk will be responsible for preparing and keeping

up to date a register of the council's property, ensuring that the property is regularly inspected and maintained and ensuring that it is covered by adequate insurance.

15. If so required by the council, the clerk will (at the cost of the council) attend training courses on subjects relevant to the role and responsibilities of the clerk of a local council.

16. If so required by the council, the clerk will prepare and issue information about the activities of the council to the press and other media organisations.

# APPENDIX 3

# DOCUMENTS AND RECORDS

A council accumulates a lot of documents and needs a system for filing current papers, storing those which should be preserved and destroying those which are no longer required.

## The legal position

A local council has custody of the "specified papers" of the parish or community.[102] These papers are defined as the public books, writings and papers of the parish or community (including photographic copies) and all documents directed by law to be kept therewith.[103]

The council has power to provide depositories for parish and community documents and may require the district or unitary council to provide a depository. Where there is no council, the district or unitary council must provide a depository.[104]

Local government electors have a right to inspect the minutes of council and, usually, committee meetings and to make copies.[105] Electors may also inspect orders for the payment of money and, at audit time, any interested person may inspect the accounts and supporting papers.[106] Local council members have a separate statutory right to inspect the council's accounts and to make copies.[107]

---

[102] s. 226, LGA 1972.
[103] s. 270(1), LGA 1972.
[104] s. 227, LGA 1972.
[105] s. 228, LGA 1972. The council is not obliged to provide copies.
[106] s. 228, LGA 1972; s. 15, ACA 1998.
[107] s. 228(3), LGA 1972.

As a general rule, it is desirable in the interests of open government and good community relations to allow interested persons, whether electors or not, to inspect any documents they please. However, due regard should be given to the need for security and, in relation to personal information about individuals, for confidentiality. Due regard must also be had for the relevant statutory controls over the disclosure of information in the Data Protection Act 1998 and the Human Rights Act 1998. The statutory provisions regarding exempt information set out in Part VA of the Local Government Act 1972 (inserted by the Local Government (Access to Information) Act 1985) do not apply to local councils as a matter of law, but there is nothing to prevent a local council from adopting them wholly or in part.

## Filing current papers

Normally, these will be kept in a filing cabinet in folders, filed according to subject matter or by number. If the number of files and folders is large, a list should be kept which is regularly updated. File names/numbers should be stated in correspondence so that letters, etc. can be assigned to their correct files and folders.

Lists of files, etc. can easily be kept on computer.

## Retention of documents

The table overleaf gives guidance on the retention of documents, based on recommendations from the Audit Commission for audit purposes.

## Appendix 3

| Document | Minimum retention period | Reason for retention |
| --- | --- | --- |
| Minute books | Indefinite | Archive/public inspection |
| Title deeds, leases agreements, contracts | Indefinite | Audit/management |
| Investments | Indefinite | Audit/management |
| Register/file of members' allowances | 6 years | Income Tax, Limitation Act |
| Scales of fees/charges | 5 years | Management |
| Receipt/payment accounts | Indefinite | Archive |
| Receipt books of all kinds | 6 years | VAT |
| Bank statements, inc. deposit/savings accounts | Last completed audit year | Audit |
| Bank paying-in books | - ditto - | Audit |
| Cheque book stubs | - ditto - | Audit |
| Quotations/tenders | 12 years/indefinite | Limitation Act |
| Paid invoices | 6 years | VAT |
| Paid cheques | 6 years | Limitation Act |
| VAT records | 6 years | VAT |
| Petty cash/postage books | 6 years | Tax, VAT, Limitation Act |
| Timesheets | Last completed audit year | Audit |
| Wages books | 12 years | Superannuation |
| Insurance policies | While valid | Management |
| Allotments registers/ plans | Indefinite | Audit/ management |

# Documents and records

### For halls, community centres, recreation grounds

Applications to hire
Lettings diaries
Copies of bills to hirers
Records of tickets issued
} 6 years      VAT

### For burial grounds

Register of fees collected
Register of burials
Register of purchased graves
Register/plan of grave spaces
Register of memorials
Application for interment
Applications for right to erect memorials
Disposal certificates
Copy certificates of grant of exclusive right of burial
} Indefinite {
Archives
Cemeteries Orders
Cremation
Regulations

*Note:* References above to the Limitation Act are to the Limitation Act 1980 (as amended). The 1980 Act sets down time limits within which court action for breach of contract, to recover damages for tortious actions and to recover land (these are the main types of action covered by the Act which are likely to be of relevance to local councils) must be started. If not started within the relevant time limit (or during any extension the court might in its discretion grant), legal action is barred.

## Planning documents

Copies of Structure Plans, Local Plans, Planning Circulars (e.g. the PPG series issued by the Department of the Environment, Transport and the Regions) should be kept as long as they are in force.

The retention of planning application papers will depend upon whether or not planning permission is granted or is refused. If permission is granted, the papers should be retained until the development is complete, including the appeal decision letter if permission is granted on appeal. If permission is refused, the papers can be destroyed once the period for lodging an appeal is over. If permission is turned down on appeal, the decision letter should be retained in case another application is made for the same site.

Planning application and decision details can readily be stored on computer. Software programs are obtainable for this purpose. Such details should be retained indefinitely, even after the papers themselves have been destroyed. The local planning authority retains all the original documentation relating to planning applications and this can be inspected if and when necessary.

## Correspondence

Correspondence relating to audit or planning matters (see above) should be retained for the same period as for other documentation. Otherwise, correspondence should be kept as long as the matter is "live", something which only the clerk is likely to be able to judge. However, if outgoing correspondence is kept on disk, the destruction of paper copies is not fatal.

## Other documentation

Documents of title and leases must be stored securely. Many councils deposit these with their bank or with solicitors.

Minute books, registers of burials and allotments and other documents which should be retained indefinitely must also be stored securely. If no longer in current use, consideration should be given to depositing them on loan at the local record office, where they will be properly looked after and will be available for inspection by the public. The same is true for other documents of historical interest which many councils have inherited or acquired, such as Tithe Awards and Inclosure Awards.

The right of the public to inspect certain documents (e.g. minute books) is not affected if the documents have been deposited at a record office.

## Review and destruction of documents

The council's documentation should be kept under regular review and weeded out as necessary.

# POWERS OF LOCAL COUNCILS

The following table sets out the main functions and powers of local councils. It is only a summary and does not contain every single power or function. Fuller details may be found in the relevant books listed in Appendix 7.

As a general rule, local councils are subject to the ordinary laws which bind the citizen. Thus, for example, a local council must obtain planning permission for material development such as the erection of buildings. In many cases, too, the exercise of a power (e.g. to place seats in the roadside) is dependent upon the council obtaining consent from the owner or occupier of the land or from the highway or other competent authority.

Where a function is marked with an asterisk, a council also has the power to give financial assistance to another person or body performing the same function.

| FUNCTION | POWERS & DUTIES | STATUTE |
|---|---|---|
| Agency arrangements | Power to arrange for the discharge of functions by another local authority | LGA 1972, s.101 |
| Allotments | Power to provide allotments. Duty to provide allotment gardens if demand exists | Smallholdings & Allotments Act 1908, ss.23, 26 & 42 |
| Baths and washhouses | Power to provide public baths and washhouses | Public Health Act 1936, ss.221-223, 227 |
| Borrowing | Power to borrow money for statutory functions | LGA 1972, Sch.13 |
| Burial grounds, cemeteries and crematoria* | Power to acquire and maintain | Open Spaces Act 1906, ss.9 & 10 |
| | Power to provide | LGA 1972, s.214 |

## Powers of local councils

| FUNCTION | POWERS & DUTIES | STATUTE |
|---|---|---|
| | Power to agree to maintain memorials and monuments | Parish Councils and Burial Authorities (Misc. Prov.) Act 1970, s.1 |
| | Power to contribute to expenses of maintaining cemeteries | LGA 1972, s.214(6) |
| Bus shelters* | Power to provide and maintain bus shelters | Local Government (Misc. Prov.) Act 1953, s.4 |
| Byelaws | Power to make byelaws for public walks and pleasure grounds | Public Health Act 1875, s.164 |
| | Cycle parks | Road Traffic Regulation Act 1984, s.57(7) |
| | Public bathing | PHA 1936, s.231 |
| | Swimming pools, bathing places, baths & washhouses | PHA 1936, s.223 |
| | Open spaces and burial grounds | OSA 1906, s.15 |
| | Hiring of pleasure boats in parks and pleasure grounds | Public Health Acts Amendment Act 1907, s.44(2); PHA 1961, s.54 |
| | Mortuaries and post-mortem rooms | PHA 1936, s.198 |
| | Dogs and dog fouling in parks and open spaces | PHA 1875, s.164; OSA 1906, s.15 |
| Charities | Power to appoint trustees of parochial charities | Charities Act 1993, s.79 |
| Clocks* | Power to provide public clocks | Parish Councils Act 1957, s.2 |
| Closed churchyards | Power (and sometimes duty) to maintain | LGA 1972, s.215 |
| Common land | Power to protect unclaimed common land from unlawful interference | Commons Registration Act 1965, s.9 |
| | Power to manage commons and village greens under a district council scheme | Commons Act 1899, ss.4 & 5 |

| FUNCTION | POWERS & DUTIES | STATUTE |
|---|---|---|
| Community centres and village halls* | Power to provide and equip premises for clubs and other athletic, social or educational organisations | LG (Misc. Prov.) Act 1976, s.19 |
| Conference facilities* | Power to provide and encourage the use of conference facilities | LGA 1972, s.144 |
| Consultation | Right to be consulted by principal councils if directed by Secretary of State (England) or by Welsh Assembly (Wales) | Local Government and Rating Act 1997, s.21; LGA 1972, s.33A |
| Crime prevention* | Power to (a) install equipment (b) establish schemes and (c) assist others in so doing for the prevention of crime | LG & RA 1997, s.31 |
| Drainage | Power to deal with ditches and ponds | PHA 1936, s.260 |
| Education | Right to appoint governors of primary schools | School Standards and Framework Act 1998, para.15 of Sch.10 |
| Entertainment and the arts* | Provision of entertainment and support for the arts | LGA 1972, s.145 |
| Flagpoles | Power to erect flagpoles in highways | Highways Act 1980, s.144 |
| "Free Resource" | Power to incur expenditure not otherwise authorised on anything which in the council's opinion is in the interests of the area or part of it or of all or some of the inhabitants | LGA 1972, s.137 |
| Gifts | Power to accept gifts | LGA 1972, s.139 |
| Highways | Power to maintain footpaths and bridleways | HA 1980, ss.43 & 50 |
| | Power to make a dedication agreement for a new highway or widening an existing highway | HA 1980, ss.30, 72 |

## Powers of local councils

| FUNCTION | POWERS & DUTIES | STATUTE |
|---|---|---|
| | Right to veto application to magistrates' court to stop up, divert or cease to maintain a public highway | HA 1980, ss.47, 116 |
| | Power to complain to local highway authority that a highway is unlawfully stopped up or obstructed | HA 1980, s.130 |
| | Power to plant trees, etc. and maintain roadside verges | HA 1980, s.96 |
| | Power to prosecute for unlawful ploughing of a footpath or bridleway | HA 1980, s.134 |
| | Power to provide traffic signs and other notices | Road Traffic Regulation Act 1984, s.72 |
| Land | Power to acquire land by by agreement, to appropriate land and to dispose of land | LGA 1972, ss.124, 126, 127 |
| | Power to acquire land by compulsory purchase | LGA 1972, s.125 |
| | Power to accept gifts of land | LGA 1972, s.139 |
| | Power to obtain particulars of persons interested in land | LG(MP)A 1976, s.16 |
| Lighting | Power to light roads and public places | PCA 1957, s.3; HA 1980, s.301 |
| Litter* | Power to provide litter bins in streets and public places | Litter Act 1983, ss.5 & 6 |
| Lotteries | Power to promote lotteries | Lotteries and Amusements Act 1976, s.7 |
| Mortuaries and post-mortem rooms | Power to provide mortuaries and post-mortem rooms | PHA 1936, s.198 |
| Nuisances* | Power to deal with offensive ponds, ditches and gutters | PHA 1936, s.260 |
| Open spaces | Power to acquire and maintain open spaces | PHA 1875, s.164; OSA 1906, ss.9, 10 |
| Parish documents | Power to give directions as to the custody of parish documents | LGA 1972, s.226 |

## Appendix 4

| FUNCTION | POWERS & DUTIES | STATUTE |
|---|---|---|
| Parking facilities | Power to provide parking places for motor vehicles and bicycles | RTRA 1984, ss.57 & 63 |
| Public buildings and village halls | Power to provide buildings for offices and for public meetings and assemblies | LGA 1972, s.133 |
| Public conveniences | Power to provide public conveniences | PHA 1936, s.87 |
| Publicity | Power to provide information about matters affecting local government | LGA 1972, s.142 |
| Records | Power to collect, exhibit and purchase local records | Local Government (Records) Act 1962, ss.1 & 2 |
| Recreation* | Power to acquire land for, or provide recreation grounds, public walks, pleasure grounds and open spaces and to manage and control them | PHA 1875, s.164; PHAAA 1890, s.44; OSA 1906, s.9 & 10; LG(MP)A 1976, s.19 |
| Seats and shelters* | Power to provide roadside seats and shelters | PCA 1957, s.1 |
| Telecommunications facilities | Power to pay BT or any other telecommunications operator any loss sustained in providing telecommunications facilities | Telecommunications Act 1984 |
| Town and country planning | Right to be notified of planning applications | Town & Country Planning Act 1990, para.8 of Sch.1; para.2 of Sch.1A (Wales) |
| Town status | Power to adopt town status | LGA 1972, ss.245, 245B |
| Tourism* | Power to contribute to encouragement of tourism | LGA 1972, s.144 |
| Traffic calming | Power to contribute to the cost of traffic calming measures | HA 1980, s.274A |
| Transport* | Power to (a) establish car-sharing schemes; (b) make grants for bus services; | LG & RA 1997, s.26 |

128

| FUNCTION | POWERS & DUTIES | STATUTE |
|---|---|---|
| | (c) provide taxi-fare concessions; (d) investigate public transport, road use and needs; (e) provide information about public transport services | |
| Village greens* | Power to maintain, to make byelaws for and to prosecute for interference with village greens | OSA 1906, s.15; Inclosure Act 1857, s.12; Commons Act 1876, s.29 |
| Village Halls* | *(see Community Centres, Public Buildings)* | |
| War memorials | Power to maintain, repair and protect war memorials | War Memorials (Local Authorities' Powers) Act 1923, s.1, as extended by LGA 1948, s.133 |
| Water supply | Power to utilise any well, spring or stream to provide facilities for obtaining water from them | PHA 1936, s.125 |

# USEFUL ADDRESSES

ACRE (Action with Communities in Rural England), Somerford Court, Somerford Road, Cheltenham, Glos GL7 1TW. (Tel: 01285 653477, Fax: 01285 654537.) Website: www.acreciro.demon.co.uk

Advisory, Conciliation and Arbitration Service (ACAS), Brandon House, 180 Borough High Street, London SE1 1LW. (Tel: 020 7396 5100.) Website: www.acas.org.uk

Association of Larger Local Councils, PO Box 191, Macclesfield, Cheshire SK11 0FG.

Audit Commission, 1 Vincent Square, London SW1P 2BR. (Tel: 020 7396 1315.) Website: www.audit-commission. gov.uk

Charity Commission, Harmsworth House Bouverie Street, London EC4Y 8DP (Head Office). Website: www.charity-commission.gov.uk

Charity Commission, Woodfield House, Tangier, Taunton TA1 4BL. ([Publications Office] Tel: 01823 345427.)

Chartered Institute of Public Finance and Accountancy (CIPFA), 3 Robert Street, London WC2N 6BH. (Tel: 020 7543 5600.) Website: www.cipfa.org.uk

Cheltenham & Gloucester College of Higher Education, Centre for Local Policy Studies, Francis Close Hall, Swindon Road, Cheltenham, Glos GL5 4AZ. (Tel: 01242 532941, Fax: 01242 543283.) Website: www.chelt.ac.uk/el/clps

Data Protection Commissioner, Wycliffe House, Water Lane,

# Useful addresses

Wilmslow, Cheshire SK9 5AF. (Tel: 01625 535777.) Website: www.dataprotection.gov.uk

Department for Education and Employment, Sanctuary Buildings, Great Smith Street, London SW1P 3BT. (Tel: 020 7925 5555, Fax: 020 7925 6971.) Website: www.dfee.gov.uk

Department of the Environment, Transport and the Regions, Eland House, Bressenden Place, London SW1E 5DU (Tel: [general enquiries] 020 7944 3000.) Website: www.detr.gov.uk

Department of Trade and Industry, 1 Victoria Street, London SW1H 0EP. (Tel: 020 7215 5000.) Website: www.dti.gov.uk

Disability Rights Commission, 7th Floor, 222 Gray's Inn Road, London WC1X 8HL. (Tel: 020 7211 3000.) Website: www.disability.gov.uk

Federation of Rural Community Councils (covering Cumbria, Durham, Lincolnshire, Northumberland, Shropshire, Staffordshire and Yorkshire), William House, Shipton Road, Skelton, York YO30 1XF. (Tel: 01904 645271, Fax: 01904 610985.)

Health and Safety Executive (Head Office), Rose Court, Ground Floor North, 2 Southwark Bridge, London SE1 9HS.

Health and Safety Executive (general information), Sheffield Information Centre, Broad Lane, Sheffield S3 7HQ. (Tel: [HSE information line] 0541 545500, Fax: 014 289 2333.) Website: www.hse.gov.uk

Inland Revenue Pension Schemes Office, Yorke House, PO Box 62, Castle Meadow Road, Nottingham NG2 1BG. (Tel: 0115 974 1713, Fax: 0115 974 1480.)

Local Councils Advisory Service, 3 Trinity Close, 20 Church Street, Henley-on-Thames, Oxon RG9 1SE. (Tel: 01491 573585, Fax: 01491 412559.)

Local Government Association (the representative body for principal authorities in England), Local Government House, Smith Square, London SW1P 3HZ. (Tel: 020 7664 3000, Fax: 020 7664 3030.) Website: www.lga.gov.uk

Local Government Commission for England, Dolphyn Court, 10/11 Great Turnstile, London WC1V 7JC. (Tel: 020 7588 1815.) Website: www.lgce.gov.uk

National Assembly for Wales, Cardiff Bay, Cardiff CF99 1NA. (Tel: 029 2089 8200 [general information] and 029 2082 5111.) Website: www.wales.gov.uk

National Association of Local Councils (the representative body for local councils), 109 Great Russell Street, London WC1B 3LD. (Tel: 020 7637 1865, Fax: 020 7436 7451.) Website: www.nalc.org.uk

National Joint Council for Local Government Services, Layden House, 76-86 Turnmill Street, London EC1M 5LG. (Tel: 020 7296 660, Fax: 020 7296 6666.) Website: www.lg-employers.gov.uk

National Playing Fields Association, 25 Ovington Square, London SW3 1LQ. (Tel: 020 7584 6445.) Website: www.npfa.co.uk

Society of Local Council Clerks, 1 Fisher Lane, Bingham, Nottingham NG13 8BQ. (Tel: 0115 923 2200, Fax: 01949 836583.) Website: www.slcc.co.uk

Stationery Office Ltd., 2nd Floor, St. Crispins, Duke Street, Norwich NR3 1PD. (National publications order line Tel: 020 7873 9090.) Website: www.hmso.gov.uk

## Useful addresses

Wales Association of Community & Town Councils, Unit 5, Betws Business Park, Park Street, Ammanford SA18 2ET. (Tel: 01269 595400.)

Welsh Local Government Association (the representative body for principal authorities in Wales), 10-11 Raleigh Walk, Atlantic Wharf, Cardiff CF1 3NQ. (Tel: 029 2046 8600, Fax: 029 2046 8601.) Website: www.wlga.org

# THE WILTSHIRE CHARTER FOR LOCAL COUNCILS

*In Chapter 5, mention is made of consultative arrangements entered into by local council and principal authorities. The Wiltshire Charter for Local Councils is an example. Permission to reproduce the Charter here has kindly been given by Wiltshire County Council.*

## Introduction

1.1   The WILTSHIRE CHARTER FOR LOCAL COUNCILS recognises and gives effect to the continuing partnership between principal councils and local councils which represent the interests of the residents, non-domestic ratepayers and other organisations of Wiltshire.

1.2   The CHARTER has been agreed between representatives of the Wiltshire Association of Local Councils and the five principal Wiltshire Councils outside Thamesdown.

1.3   The CHARTER will provide the basis for effective consultation between the principal councils and parish and town councils (local councils) and offers the opportunity for local councils, if they wish, to have greater involvement in the provision of services for local people.

1.4   Under the provisions of the CHARTER, the principal councils and the local councils will work together to develop an effective partnership governing the future conduct of matters between elected members and officials of the principal and local councils in Wiltshire.

## General

1.5  The CHARTER acknowledges and gives due weight to the important but separate roles and functions carried out by each democratically elected tier of local government as outlined below:

- Principal councils will operate at the strategic and local level to ensure that competing needs and interests are balanced in an even-handed way in order to achieve the equitable distribution of services throughout their areas and to protect minority communities and special needs or interests.

- Local councils will operate at the very local level to promote the interests of the residents of their respective villages, towns and communities.

1.6  The CHARTER recognises that it is important for the strategic and local tiers of local government to operate together in order to secure the effective response to the needs and aspirations of all Wiltshire's people.

1.7  Local councils will endeavour, wherever possible, to provide the principal council with an assessment of the needs and wishes of residents of individual communities. For their part, the principal councils will undertake to take account of those local needs and inform local councils of wider strategic issues affecting those communities.

1.8  As well as matters relating to the general social, economic, and environmental well-being of local communities, the principal councils and local councils will actively consult over the planning and monitoring of the full range of local government services in each area. These matters are set out in more detail under CONSULTATION below.

1.9 The CHARTER will commit the principal councils and the local councils to the provision of information and other support to enable local electors within unparished areas (or parished areas without councils) of the County to:

- seek the parishing of their area where there is local support; and

- to establish parish, town or neighbourhood councils where these currently do not exist.

1.10 The principal and local councils agree that wherever possible elections to local and principal councils should be held at the same time in order to stimulate increased electoral activity and minimise costs to local councils.

## Relationships between principal councils and local councils

1.11 The principal councils and the local councils believe that that it is important for principal councillors to maintain a close relationship with local councils in their wards.

1.12 The pressures on time of elected members are recognised, but principal councils will:

- encourage councillors to accept invitations to attend meetings of local councils in their wards or divisions whenever possible; and

- send copies of correspondence on any significant matter with local councils to principal councillors representing that area.

1.13 The local councils will:

- invite the principal councillor(s) for the area to meetings of the local council;

- at the local council's discretion, allow them to speak at such meetings;

- provide, on request, to the principal councillor(s) for the area agendas, reports and minutes of meetings of the local council; and

- help to keep the principal councillor(s) for the area informed about local views on any matter relating to the principal councils' responsibilities.

## Consultation

1.14 The principal councils will undertake to consult directly with individual local councils over matters specifically relating to their town, village or community. Such matters will include local planning applications and proposals for traffic management schemes. A list of issues which will be automatically referred to local councils for consideration is attached as SCHEDULE ONE.

1.15 At the time of consultation the principal councils will provide information and reasons for any proposals they are suggesting.

1.16 The principal councils wish to give local councils every reasonable opportunity to comment on and influence decisions to be made by them on their proposals which may affect the local community.

1.17 Within the constraints imposed by statute, necessary service and committee timetables and any special agency requirements, the principal councils will allow local councils a reasonable time for comment. Local councils will, for their part, respond as promptly as possible and within any reasonable timescales set by the principal councils.

1.18 The principal councils reserve the right under this statement to withhold information defined as "exempt" or "confidential" under the Local Government (Access to Information) Act 1985: this right shall also apply to local councils.

1.19 The principal councils will also consult with local councils on strategic service matters having an impact on individual parish and town councils and their surrounding communities.

1.20 To enable effective consultation to be carried out, the principal councils and the local councils will conform to a code of conduct governing consultation procedures, as follows:

The principal councils will undertake to:

- provide all relevant information on which the local council is being asked to provide a view;

- provide a realistic consultation period in which to respond;

- give a commitment that the views of local councils will be taken into account and where a decision falls to be made by a committee or sub-committee of the principal council the views of the local council shall be fully reported; and

- provide an explanation if the decision does not accord with local views.

The local councils, while recognising the authority of the principal council to make the final decision, will:

- provide a practical and realistic response to the matter under consideration;

- provide a response within the specified consultation period; and

- enter into a constructive dialogue, when necessary, to air different views.

1.21 In view of the particular local impact of planning applications the following code of conduct is agreed by principal and local councils to govern the consultation arrangements relating to development control matters:

The principal councils will:

- notify the local council of all planning applications received in respect of their parish;

- allow 21 days for the submission of representation by the local council (the statutory minimum is 14 days);

- notify the local council of any significant amendment to a planning application, and provide an opportunity for representations to be made before a decision is taken on the amended plan;

- undertake to ensure that where the local council's recommendation or view differs from the action proposed by the principal council's chief planning officer under delegated authority, the matter shall be referred to the principal council's development control committee;

- where a matter falls to be decided by a principal council's development control committee or sub-committee, undertake to ensure that the local council's representations shall be reported fully to that committee;

- upon request, provide the local council with copies of development control committee agendas, minutes and decision notices in respect of their area together with a written explanation of any decision which is contrary to the view of the local council; and

- provide (in collaboration with the Wiltshire Association of Local Councils where appropriate) training courses for local councillors to aid an understanding of the planning process and the matters which have a material bearing upon the determination of a planning application.

The local council will endeavour:

- to acknowledge that the principal council will not always be able to accede to the requests of local councils;

- to respond promptly in writing to all planning applications received from principal councils;

- to specify as fully as possible the reasons for an objection to, or support for, a particular planning application;

- to create a mechanism whereby the local council can respond to any amended plans received from the principal council; and

- to report, should they so choose, any breaches of the Town and Country Planning legislation.

1.22 Nothing in the above paragraph will diminish the commitment to enhance the consultative relationship between local and principal councils in respect of the other matters set out in SCHEDULE ONE, although these will have to be the subject of further discussion as to the precise way in which consultation will take place.

1.23 The consultative arrangements set out above shall be the subject of joint periodic review.

## Enhancing the powers and influence of local councils

1.24 The CHARTER will create the means by which new initiatives for the provision of services which are the responsibility of the principal councils, may be established and which may be entered into by local councils on a voluntary basis and within the limitations imposed by compulsory competitive tendering legislation, as follows:

- AGENCY AGREEMENTS between principal councils and other individual local councils, or consortia of local councils, enabling services which are the responsibility of the principal councils to be directly provided by local council(s);

- COMMUNITY PARTNERSHIP VENTURES enabling services provided by the principal councils to be enhanced or supplemented using resources provided by the local council.

1.25 The principal councils will also arrange to provide some services and technical assistance to the local councils in order to support the local provision of services for which the principal councils have a statutory responsibility.

1.26 The principal councils recognise that the larger local councils may have the capability and desire to seek

Appendix 6

further agency powers that are not suggested in this paper. In such cases the principal councils will undertake to consider any such proposals and, bearing in mind the principles set out below, endeavour wherever practicable to enable those aspirations to be realised.

1.27 The principal councils will undertake (in collaboration with the Wiltshire Association of Local Councils where appropriate) to provide periodic training courses for local councillors to aid an understanding of the services and functions of the principal councils.

## Agency agreements

1.28 As indicated above, the CHARTER acknowledges the statutory roles and responsibilities of the strategic and local tiers of local government in Wiltshire in the provision of local services.

1.29 However, the principal councils will also recognise the benefits to be gained from arrangements for enabling certain services for which it is responsible to be provided by a local council acting as its agent. A list of services which could be made available as AGENCY AGREEMENTS is attached as SCHEDULE TWO.

1.30 Whilst it is acknowledged that AGENCY ARRANGEMENTS should be available, the principal councils and the local councils agree that any agency arrangements should be introduced only after consideration of the following key principles:

- the need to provide the best value for money for the residents of Wiltshire and individual parishes;

- the need to provide a consistent approach across the area of the principal council;

- the effect the agency work would have on the workload of local councils, their clerks and other staff;

- the need to meet any prescribed minimum level of service provision; and

- the effect on the remainder of the service if some work is undertaken by the local council as their agent.

1.31 Should a request for an AGENCY AGREEMENT satisfy the above principles the principal council and the local councils will agree to abide by a code of conduct governing AGENCY AGREEMENTS, as set out below:

The principal council will:

- supply a list of services which the local councils may elect to provide within their town, village or community;

- provide detailed information of the requirements of the service and set clear minimum standards for its level of provision and quality;

- allocate the necessary level of funding to enable the service to be provided to that minimum standard;

- allow the local council to provide the service in a style and a manner which accords with local needs, and for the service voluntarily to be improved or extended over and above the minimum standard, drawing on funding from the local precept; and

- provide an explanation if an application for an AGENCY AGREEMENT is turned down.

Local councils to act as agents will:

- provide the service as efficiently and effectively as possible and at least to the minimum standards laid down by the principal council, for the duration of the agreement;

- render proper accounts to the principal council for expenditure on the service, excluding any enhancements, and provide the necessary information for the principal authority to monitor the service delivery.

1.32 The AGENCY AGREEMENT will be subject to regular review by both parties, covering standards set and funding allowed for the service.

## Community partnership ventures

1.33 Some local councils will not wish, or feel they have the capacity, to become agents. Indeed, this was a main finding of the Parish Survey undertaken by Wiltshire County Council in 1992. In such cases local councils may still assume a more active role in the provision of principal council services in their own areas.

1.34 In such circumstances, the local council may enter into a COMMUNITY PARTNERSHIP VENTURE with the principal council to ensure that services provided in the local area are of high standard and responsive to local needs.

1.35 There are two forms of COMMUNITY PARTNERSHIP VENTURE:

- The local enhancement of services.

  This will entail arrangements whereby services which are the responsibility of the principal councils and run by those councils are enhanced or extended using the resources of the local council. For example, library opening hours could be extended beyond normal opening or services enhanced, drawing on funding from the local precept provided by the local council.

- Local service specification.

  This will entail local councils reviewing the particular needs of their communities and providing to the principal councils details of local priority needs. The principal councils will then undertake to take account of those local priorities within the existing service specification. However, no additional expenditure could be incurred in the area overall unless the local council agreed to fund this extra service from the local precept, or the principal council considers there to be special justification for so doing (such as the closure of military bases, etc.).

1.36 Examples of services which could be the subject of COMMUNITY PARTNERSHIP VENTURES are attached as SCHEDULE THREE.

1.37 Principal councils and local councils will agree to abide by a code of conduct governing COMMUNITY PARTNERSHIP VENTURES as set out below:

The principal council will:

- provide advice to local councils preparing local needs surveys;

- provide technical assistance to local councils preparing COMMUNITY PARTNERSHIP VENTURES;

- provide sufficient information relating to the services provided in the area to allow the local councils to form views upon their responsiveness to local needs;

- accommodate the wishes of local councils wherever service enhancement is practicable; and

- involve local councils in the periodic review of the services in order that they may remain responsive to local needs.

Local councils will have the opportunity to:

- co-ordinate local needs surveys in conjunction with principal councils;

- apply for COMMUNITY PARTNERSHIP VENTURES based upon their own requirements and aspirations;

- participate in the periodic review of principal council services; and

- collect local views over the performance of services and provide these for performance review and service monitoring purposes.

1.38 As with AGENCY AGREEMENTS, a formal service level agreement will be required relating to the funding to be provided and how the service will be improved. This will also be subject to regular review by both parties.

## Area forums

1.39 The principal and local councils will consider the possibility of creating area based forums of local and principal councillors as a means of exchanging views upon matters of strategic importance. Such area forums could be based upon the 19 community areas in Wiltshire. Further discussions will be required to establish the possible form and functions of AREA FORUMS.

## Appeals

1.40 In the event of disagreement between a principal and a local council regarding the operation of the CHARTER the matter shall be referred to a panel of members of the principal council, representatives of the Wiltshire Association of Local Councils, and members of the local council concerned. The Panel shall consider the matter and make a recommendation to the principal council. The principal council shall have the final decision upon the complaint and shall furnish the local council with a written explanation of its decision.

## *SCHEDULE ONE*

### Issues on which the principal council will consult local councils directly

Drainage plans

Footpath orders

Tree preservation/woodland orders

Designation of conservation areas and environmental schemes

Traffic management schemes, traffic regulation orders

Criteria for allocating housing, particularly for special needs

Public entertainment and other local licences

Applications for planning permission, listed building consent, conservation area demolitions

Applications for telecommunications equipment

The provision of civic amenity sites

Proposals for the reorganisation of schools

Proposals for changes in the opening hours of local libraries

Provision of mobile libraries' service

Significant changes to local community education/
leisure facilities

Policies for pollution monitoring

Arrangements to be made for dog control

Provision or withdrawal of local information centres

Provision or withdrawal from permanent use of public
conveniences

Proposals for amendments to or provision of new
recycling facilities

Provision of new car parking facilities or changes in
permitted waiting periods

Emergency planning arrangements within individual
parishes

**SCHEDULE TWO**

**Services which may be offered to local councils on an
agency basis**

Management of temporary and permanent markets

Licensing of street traders

Management of off-street car parking*

Street cleaning, litter collection and monitoring of fly
tipping*

Licensing of street and door to door collections

Street naming

Management of parks, open spaces, gardens, village
greens, play areas, recreation grounds, picnic sites,
and maintenance of road verges*

Management of public toilets*

Footpath management, including maintenance, waymarking and removal of obstructions*

Management of bus shelters and maintenance of transport information*

Administration of transport schemes and concessionary fares permits

Management of school crossing patrols

Road safety initiatives including cycle and motorcycle training

Organisation of local programmes of events, festivals and carnivals*

Management of community halls and centres*

Lettings of buildings and grounds owned by the principal council (except schools, where lettings are the responsibility of the governing body, or where for operational reasons it is not practicable)

Local environmental management – monitoring of the local area for such problems as abandoned cars, potholes and footway hazards, sign cleaning, management of local recycling points

*\* Local councils already have certain statutory powers for such functions; the list is intended to refer to facilities provided by the principal council.*

## SCHEDULE THREE

### Services which could be the subject of community partnership ventures

Local highways improvements*

Traffic calming initiatives

Additional footpath lighting*

Local crime prevention or fire safety initiatives

Street cleaning, litter collection and monitoring of fly tipping*

Maintenance of parks, open spaces, gardens, village greens, play areas, recreation grounds, picnic sites and road verges*

Management of public toilets*

Footpath management including maintenance, waymarking and removal of obstructions*

Localised winter maintenance and control of grit bins

Management of bus shelters and maintenance of transport information*

Road safety initiatives including cycle and motorcycle training

Organisation of local programmes of events, festivals and carnivals*

Management of community halls and centres*

Lettings of buildings and grounds owned by the principal council (except schools, where lettings are the responsibility of the governing body, or where for operational reasons it is not practicable)

Local environmental enhancement schemes

Local environmental management – monitoring of the local area for such problems as abandoned cars, potholes and footway hazards, sign cleaning, management of local recycling points*

*\* Local councils already have certain statutory powers for such functions; the list is intended to refer to facilities provided by the principal council.*

# FURTHER READING

*Local Council Administration* by Charles Arnold-Baker OBE (5th Edition, 1997), Butterworths, 35 Chancery Lane, London WC2A 1EL.

*The Parish Councillor's Guide* by John Prophet (17th Edition, 2000), Shaw & Sons Ltd., Shaway House, 21 Bourne Park, Bourne Road, Crayford, Kent DA1 4BZ (Tel: 01322 621100, Fax: 01322 550553). Website: www.shaws.co.uk

*Co-operation between Local Councils and Principal Authorities* by Paul Clayden, Local Councils Advisory Service, 3 Trinity Close, 20 Church Street, Henley-on-Thames, Oxon. RG9 1SE.

*How to be a Better Councillor* by Paul Clayden.

*How to be a Better Clerk* by Paul Clayden.

*Local Council Finance* by Ron Harrop, Shaw and Sons Ltd.

*Local Council Finance Best Practice Guide* by Ron Harrop, Laurie Howes and Elisabeth Skinner, Centre for Policy Studies, Cheltenham and Gloucester College of Higher Education, Francis Close Hall, Swindon Road, Cheltenham GL50 4AZ.

*Working for Your Parish* (5 guides on Law for Local Councils, Procedures for Local Councils, Town and Country Planning, Community and Environmental Action, Local Council Finance Best Practice Guide), Cheltenham and Gloucester College of Higher Education.

*Powers and Constitution of Local Councils*, The National

Association of Local Councils, 109 Great Russell Street, London WC1B 3LD.

*Standing Orders and Chairmanship*, The National Association of Local Councils.

*The Clerk's Manual*, Society of Local Council Clerks, 1 Fisher Lane, Bingham, Nottingham NG13 8BQ (available to members only).

## Magazines and periodicals

*Clerks and Councils Direct* (bi-monthly), PO Box 276, Ashford, Kent TN23 1ZU.

*The Clerk* (quarterly), Society of Local Council Clerks.

*Local Council Review* (bi-monthly), The National Association of Local Councils.

# PARTS III, IV AND V OF THE LOCAL GOVERNMENT ACT 2000

## *INTRODUCTION*

The Local Government Act 2000 received the Royal Assent on 28th July 2000 and is being brought into force in stages. It is divided into six parts, dealing respectively with: (I) promotion of economic, social or environmental well being etc; (II) arrangements with respect to executives etc; (III) conduct of local government members and employees; (IV) elections; (V) miscellaneous and (VI) supplementary. Parts I and II do not apply to local councils and only parts of Part V. Part VI deals with order making powers, commencement and other consequential matters. This appendix covers only Parts III, IV and V.

The Act is being brought into force in stages. Parts III, IV and V are likely to be brought into force during 2001.

Unless otherwise indicated, a reference to the Secretary of State includes a reference to the National Assembly for Wales.

## *PART III – CONDUCT OF LOCAL GOVERNMENT MEMBERS AND EMPLOYEES*

Part III will affect all levels of local authorities, including local councils. The Secretary of State is given power to specify principles which are to govern the conduct of members and co-opted members of local authorities. (Consultation on these principles is already taking place.) He is also empowered to issue a model code of conduct for such members (which will replace the current National Code of Local Government Conduct issued in 1990). Some parts of the model code will be mandatory. These are likely to be provisions which will supersede sections 94-98 of the Local Government Act 1972 (restrictions on voting on account of pecuniary interests), to be repealed when the new code comes into force.

Local authorities will be required to adopt a code of conduct, no doubt based largely on the model code. This will be a new requirement for local councils, which have hitherto been bound by sections 94-98 of the LGA 1972 and the National Code of Local Government Conduct without any need to adopt them.

Members of local authorities will be required to give a written undertaking to comply with the authority's adopted code. This is likely to be incorporated into the declaration of acceptance of office which all those elected or co-opted as councillors must sign. Failure to sign the declaration at the proper time will result in vacation of office.

The conduct of members will be policed by standards committees and a Standards Board. Principal authorities will be required to establish standards committees, the general functions of which will be to promote and maintain high standards of conduct and to assist members in complying with the code of conduct. The standards committees will also be responsible for overseeing the conduct of parish and community councils within the area of the relevant principal council.

In England, a Standards Board will be established with the principal function of investigating complaints against members of local authorities (including local councils) who are alleged to have broken their authority's code of conduct. In Wales, the same functions will be performed by the

Commission for Local Administration in Wales (i.e. the Welsh Local Government Ombudsman). In both England and Wales, the Local Government Ombudsmen will continue to deal with complaints of maladministration by principal councils (local councils are not subject to the jurisdiction of the Ombudsmen).

An elaborate procedure is laid down for dealing with, and adjudicating on, complaints. If a complaint is upheld, the case tribunal hearing the complaint may (1) decide to take no disciplinary action, or (2) suspend or partially suspend the member from the relevant authority, or (3) disqualify the member from being or becoming a member of that, or any other, authority. Partial suspension will occur where the member is prevented from exercising particular functions or having particular responsibilities. Suspension can be for up to one year or until the member's term of office expires (if shorter). Disqualification can be for up to five years.

The monitoring officer of each relevant authority must establish and maintain a register of interests of members and co-opted members of the authority. Local councils are not required to appoint monitoring officers, and it will be the duty of the monitoring officer for the appropriate principal authority to keep the register of interests of members of local councils. The interests which must be registered will be set out in the mandatory provisions in the model code of conduct and will replace the current requirement for local councils to keep a register of pecuniary interests (section 96 of the LGA 1972).

The Secretary of State is given power to issue a code of conduct for "qualifying employees" of relevant authorities (including local councils). Such employees will be specified in the regulations which comprise the code of conduct.

## PART IV – ELECTIONS

Part IV givers the Secretary of State power to specify a scheme of elections for principal councils, being one of three schemes set out in the Act:

(1) A four-year term of office for councillors; elections every four years; all councillors elected at the same time; all councillors retire together.

(2) A four-year term of office for councillors; elections every two years; half the councillors elected every two years; half the councillors retire in each election year.

(3) A four-year term of office for councillors; elections every year except every third year; one third of the councillors elected in each election year; one third of councillors retire in each election year.

The Secretary of State is also given power to vary local council election timetables in the light of the election scheme operated by the relevant principal council.

## PART V – MISCELLANEOUS

Part V abolishes the powers of the auditor to seek a declaration from the court that an item of account is unlawful and to seek recovery of amounts not accounted for or unlawfully spent (i.e. the power of surcharge). Also abolished is the power of the auditor to issue a prohibition order to prevent the incurring of unlawful expenditure. This power is replaced by a power to issue an advisory notice, if the auditor believes that a council is about to make a decision which would result in unlawful expenditure or to cause loss or deficiency. The effect of such a notice is to make unlawful the implementation of the decision, unless the council has taken into account the reasons given by the auditor for issuing the notice and has told the auditor of its intention to implement the decision.

The Act thus repeals the auditor's special powers to control unlawful expenditure, but leaves unaltered his power to seek judicial review if he believes that a council has incurred unlawful expenditure or the like (section 24 of the Audit Commission Act 1998).

Local authorities (including local councils) are given a new power to make payments, or provide other benefits, to persons who have suffered as a result of their maladministration.

The Secretary of State is given power to amend the relevant provisions in Schedule 12 of the LGA 1972 so as to substitute some other period greater than three clear days for the giving of notice of the meetings of principal councils.

The Secretary of State is given power to make regulations about allowances for parish and community councillors. In due course, this power is likely to supersede the powers contained in sections 173-178 of the LGA 1972.